FAITH WHILE WAITING

VISIONARY: Juanita N. Woodson
CO-AUTHORS:
Cyteese Alexander
Lisa Freeman
Cystal D. Harrison M.Ed.
Jay T. Harrison, Sr.
Marvastine Nichols
Josias Jean-Pierre
Verenda K. Cobbs
Demetria Williams
Philomena Whitehead
Tanisha Graves
Lisa Seymour
Tonya B. Bailey

Faith While Waiting

Copyright © 2024 by Juanita N. Woodson,
Cyteese Alexander
Lisa Freeman
Cystal D. Harrison M.Ed
Jay T. Harrison, Sr.
Marvastine Nichols
Josias Jean-Pierre
Verenda K. Cobbs
Demetria Williams
Philomena Whitehead
Tanisha Graves
Lisa Seymour
Tonya B. Bailey

Published by Grace 4 Purpose, Publishing Co. LLC

All rights reserved. No part of this publication may be reproduced in any form or by any electronic or mechanical means, including information storage and retrieval systems, without prior permission in writing from the publisher, except by reviewers, who may quote brief passages in a review.

All scripture quotations, unless otherwise indicated, are taken from the King James Version of the Bible, unless otherwise indicated. All rights reserved.

ISBN: **979-8-9908003-3-5**

Editing by: Grace 4 Purpose, Publishing Co. LLC

Book cover design by Grace 4 Purpose, Publishing Co. LLC

Printed and bound in the United States of America

DEDICATION

This book is dedicated to anyone who is in a season of waiting. Remember that God never wastes a season…even a waiting season.

TABLE OF CONTENTS

Introduction..3
Chapter One: Cyteese Alexander...4
Chapter Two: Lisa Freeman..12
Chapter Three: Cystal D. Harrison.....................................24
Chapter Four: Marvastine Nichols.....................................35
Chapter Five: Josias Jean-Pierre......................................43
Chapter Six: Verenda K. Cobbs...52
Chapter Seven: Demetria Williams....................................67
Chapter Eight: Philomena Whitehead................................77
Chapter Nine: Jay T. Harrison, Sr.....................................85
Chapter Ten: Tanisha Graves..99
Chapter Eleven: Lisa Seymour..109
Chapter Twelve: Tonya B. Bailey.....................................117
Chapter Thirteen: Juanita N. Woodson............................124

"Patience is not the ability to wait, but how you act while you're waiting."

– Joyce Meyer

Introduction

Waiting is never easy. It's in those moments of uncertainty, when answers seem far away and prayers go unanswered, that our faith is truly tested. *Faith While Waiting* is a heartfelt collection of stories, reflections, and experiences from people just like you who have walked through their own seasons of waiting. This anthology is a reminder that waiting isn't about standing still—it's about holding onto hope, trusting God's timing, and allowing Him to work in our hearts. Each story will encourage you to keep believing, even when the answers don't come right away, and to embrace the growth that happens in the in-between.

Chapter One
Cyteese Alexander

Miracles

As the body without the spirit is dead, so faith without deeds is dead.
--James 2:26 NIV

Faith and Patience, I know it sounds like a lot, right? At times it can be hard to maintain when facing challenges. However, I am a firm believer and witness that you can maintain both faith and patience when faced with unexpected challenges. Patience while waiting with faith can look like hearing a promise from God and then years going by and you are still waiting to see the promise. In the natural, you can't see anything, but it does look different when you look at it spiritually.

I had to put my faith to work when my baby was born prematurely and faced complications. I remember that I was given a promise that He would live. I held on to that promise no matter what the doctors or tests showed. The patience that I needed to see his healing in the natural came easier when I stayed in God's presence and sought after His face. Now I will not lie, waiting can take a toll on your mental and emotional state, especially when it is about your child's life. I didn't say everyday was a good day, there were times that I saw him lying in the hospital bed and going through multiple surgeries all because the condition was not changing. I was on an emotional rollercoaster because what I saw in the natural did not match the promise that God had given me for my son's life.

Faith While Waiting

We often think that when God gives us a promise that it will come the next day, or the next week. We want it to happen quickly. Sometimes it does happen immediately, but there are times when waiting is necessary. It can be months or even years before that promise comes to pass. What I have learned after being in the waiting room is that you can't rush God. I also learned that there were some things that he needed me to do and learn while in the waiting room. The best thing I could have done was stay in the face of God to direct me and so that I could hear clearly.

Now let me make this clear even though I prayed and continued to ask God what I should be doing during this time, it does not mean that being in the waiting room was smooth sailing It was not. The frustrations that I encountered were real. At one point I found myself getting mad with God. The doubt started creeping in, and I started to question if I heard right and that it was actually Him speaking to me. God showed me that He was with my son and that His promised stands, my son is still here and healed today.

There were many other obstacles and challenges that I've faced in my life. Losing jobs, income, and family medical emergencies. At times it has felt like one thing after another one. It looked like the enemy just came and set up camp in my home, and that was something else I had to encounter. I had to learn to keep my eyes on the main thing and that was the promise of God. After the experience that I faced with my son when he was born and how God kept His promise then, I knew that He would always be with me no matter what challenges came my way.
I know they say pray about everything (which you are supposed to do) but you also may have to do more than just pray. The scripture James 2:26 reminds us that "FAITH WITHOUT WORKS IS DEAD". We can

have all the faith, and we can pray all the prayers, but there will come a time where we must do some work. I knew in order for me to maintain my faith I needed to start taking sone steps to do the work. I started therapy, I also started doing some inner work and healing. This really helped me because my mind was no longer focused on the "when" while waiting. My mindset shifted and started to focus more on the work that I was putting in and that helped me to not get frustrated as quickly when I didn't see things happening quickly.

My faith was tested again in 2023 when my sister, nieces, nephew, and bother in law were in a very bad car accident. Not only did we have to wait to get answers, we had to wait for the long surgeries, we also did not know where my sister was initially. All I could do was pray, and walk around yet another waiting room pleading the blood of Jesus over their lives. And even though my faith was tested hard, it also evolved. I was able to see the evidence of God's hand at work. The healing power that took place was all God! Even though some of them are still going through healing, I still trust that even in the waiting period "ALL IS WELL". Seeing the miraculous things that took place made my level of faith go up more.

One of my favorite scriptures that I hold on to so tightly is "BE STILL AND KNOW THAT I AM GOD". (Psalm 46: 10) That scripture speaks to me so much in seasons of waiting. Even though it says to be still it's not saying to not do anything. I understand from that scripture that I need to quiet my mind, my inner thoughts, my anxiety, and anything else that tries to come and place fear and doubt. Quiet the noise and let God do what only He can do.

Faith While Waiting

When God begins to put things back together in your life, things that you thought could never be fixed, and He will bring you back to a place that was even better than before. That is one of the most amazing moments when you are in that waiting season. You will see relationships being mended; you will see first-hand the healing that you prayed for being done right before your eyes. That was a revelation that sparked in me that I had to ask myself these questions, "why do I doubt God? Why do I think that what I go through is too hard for Him? Why do I put Him in a box like He is ordinary when there is nothing ordinary about Him?" He is more than that and, in that moment, I started walking, thinking, and speaking differently.

The outcome of the situation was not what I was expecting and how I thought it should be. But it still turned out the way God wanted it to be in that moment. Yes, you read it correctly that even though it was not what I was expecting it is still "well" because my faith has increased, and I know there is always a reason behind what God does. He still has a purpose and plan and all I can do is trust that.

My growth has really taken off. I am so proud of myself because I have come so far in my walk with God and faith. The challenges and hardships that we face are not supposed to come to break you, they are there to come to strengthen you, your walk and anything else that God wants to do. My experiences have impacted my journey and my faith in the waiting seasons in such a positive way.

1. **TRUST THE PROCESS.** Yes, I know it is something that is said and heard a lot but I didn't know the depths of that saying until I had to go through it and saw first-hand the hand of God moving. While you are in that season of waiting, keep working, keep moving, pray and ask the father to silence any doubt, naysayers, and negative thinking etc. Lay at the feet of Jesus. What will move the hand of God quicker and that is pleasing in the sight of God is when you can show Him that you trust Him. Yes it is okay to cry through the process, but I learned crying about the problem was not going to make Him move any faster Him. It is our faith that moves God. Cry, but don't stay there.

2. **READ THE WORD OF GOD.** It is important to stay connected to your Word in ALL times. You can maintain your faith and patience by reading the Word of God, fasting, praying and listening to your favorite gospel songs or encouraging songs that help you while you are waiting on Him.

Cyteese Alexander

Cyteese Alexander is a wife, and a mother of 4 children. Her journey started different from others; she was a high-school dropout but that did not stop her. She went back and received her GED after giving birth to her first three children. Cyteese is a minister, motivational speaker and a 4x published author; one of which is an Amazon Best-Seller. She has also been nominated 2 years in a row for the ACHI magazine awards. Cyteese is continuing to walk in her purpose and dreams. She has made a commitment to fulfill all that God has put her on this earth to do.

Contact Information:

To book a speaking engagement or to connect on other projects.

Facebook: Cyteese Alexander
Instagram: @Iam_cyteese
Email: iamcyteese@gmail.com

Be on the lookout for the relaunch of her website iamcyteese.com

Faith While Waiting

"But those who wait on the Lord will renew their strength. They will soar on wings like eagles; they will run and not grow weary, they will walk and not be faint."

– Isaiah 40:31

Chapter Two

Lisa Freeman
Released to Rest

"God never said that the journey would be easy, but He did say that the arrival would be worthwhile."
- Max Lucado

Walking by faith is literally my life. Once I learned what faith really meant I began to exercise it over everything. The day I decided to release what I consider the worst pain in my adult life is the day I feel like God knew I trusted Him like never before. I didn't realize how this one situation held me back yet ended up being the catalyst of me experiencing the unexplainable! Grief was tugging at my emotions but my faith and trust in God had my heart. Before I share this story with you, allow me to share a few things about my faith walk.

Faith is described as trust and confidence in God and His promises, even when they are not yet seen or fully understood. One of the clearest definitions of faith can be found in Hebrews 11:1 KJV which states, "Now faith is the substance of things hoped for, the evidence of things not seen." I exercised my faith to develop my relationship with God and to help me discover myself! Without this leading my life I would not have been able to accomplish the roles and responsibilities of my life.

My mantra and goal in life is to, "Live everyday like it's a gift from God." I try to look at each day I wake up as an opportunity to enjoy freedom, peace and be joyful so that I can really enjoy life carefree. I count it a privilege to wake up and experience things like grace and favor. I want to be able to live and leave a legacy that I lived the life God wanted me to live. The only way I know how to do that is by Faith.

I released my faith with great expectancy for a happy marriage and by exercising the Word, creating boundaries and being in agreement with my husband on our marital goals, we are living the life we have created together beautifully. I released my Faith from "mommy mode" to watching my children evolve into the grown men and women they have become. It can become very taxing on your mental health trying to do life without leaning on the Word of God especially as parents because sometimes we have to sit back and allow them to go through things we really want to save them from. Along with motherhood, my entrepreneurial journey is another facet of my life where I am constantly releasing my faith. I decided to become a full-time entrepreneur years ago to now having several entities that I manage.

To know what I know now in this seasoned lifestyle, Faith involves believing in and hoping for things that may not be visible or tangible at the moment. Just because you don't see it doesn't mean it can't be done. The pattern God continues to show me has been an absolute fact that with Him all things are possible. Matthew 19:26 KJV

When I decided to write my first book, "BE the Change, Breaking Limitations & Pursuing Confidence for Bigger & Better" it was something I had been journaling about for about 10 years. I knew I wanted to share my story but I just didn't know how to make it happen. Time passed, seasons changed, and God placed the right people in my life and my desire became a reality. The stories that I shared in my book are of life lessons that helped me to pursue change which also led to God using those situations to actually bless my life and career. Sometimes the hardest trials are the very ones that God wants to use so that someone else can find their deliverance. I also shared stories from my past that exposed some things but it's my story and journey, it made me evolve into the faithful woman I am today. Even if no one stands with you, stand with God! That's what Faith is all about, believing in God's truth and promises, trusting Him completely and living out that trust in everyday actions, even when circumstances are uncertain.

In December 2020, I made the announcement that I was retiring from being a hairstylist. It was my 25th year in the industry and I felt like the timing was sufficient for me to let it go and fully pursue my other businesses full-time. It was also a very sensitive time in my life because I was mentally suffering from the loss of my Dad earlier that year. I was emotionally unbalanced, overwhelmed, angry, and severely hurt by my family; all while at the same time still trying to show up for my family and my clients. I was an emotional wreck and did not realize that what I needed the most was to allow myself to heal.

All I knew was I had to keep showing up because I am a business owner and my businesses would fail if I didn't keep showing up, so I toughed it out. I put on the mask and made myself look all right. I switched up my responsibility to make it seem like I was still in control but emotionally I was just getting by mentally day by day. Some days I felt like I wasn't going to make it. I simply wanted to shut everything down and do nothing. I was really at a point in my life where I knew if I did not get help with my responsibilities I would not have been able to navigate through all the emotional pain I was experiencing with the loss of my Dad.

Faith While Waiting

So that's what I decided to do. I hired a lawyer to assist with my responsibilities concerning my Dad and made a decision to distance myself from anybody who was not aligning themselves with my sanity. I became very guarded and distant with those I felt had contributed to my suffering. One thing I had to embrace was that it was absolutely okay to not be (emotionally) okay… because I needed to accept the fact that I was grieving. I was so torn about trying to show up for my businesses and emotionally overwhelmed. I had to teach myself that for once I cannot fix or change the way people felt about me. But the type of person I am, I despise leaving things undone. So I had to exercise my faith to let go and let God help me to not take things personally. I want to be transparent with you about this because if what I am about to share will help someone else believe God just one more time then I will have done my good work.

There were family members who hurt me to the core of my heart. I was devastated, emotionally traumatized and at one point felt like I couldn't forgive them. But God knew what was happening to me. When I relinquished some of that responsibility I had on my shoulders, it opened up some time for me to heal. I constantly had to choose to believe God was going to help me heal. One thing I remembered feeling was "fear", fear that I wouldn't forgive, fear that I would miss God, fear that I couldn't heal because I was grieving my Dad so much. All I knew was I needed help, that help came when I constantly kept surrendering my thoughts over to God in prayer and journaling. Eventually God sent help by way of people that would help and assist with the responsibilities I had as the Administrator of my Dad's estate.

Faith While Waiting

I would say around 2022, two years had passed and my Dad's estate was finalized. I remembered feeling a partial sense of relief but there was still some lingering emotional distress I was feeling every time I thought about having to face my family members. I had made an executive decision for myself and sanity that since my Dad's estate was legally closed I now no longer wanted or needed a relationship with them. At this moment I felt like I needed to do this for myself. I needed to heal, I needed to validate my own self, I needed to know that it was worth standing up for myself and I owed it to myself to heal. You cannot properly heal feeling guilty. It's just like having an open wound, watching yourself bleed expecting to be healed, but doing nothing to stop the bleeding. Guilt makes you stagnant, guilt only thrives in your thoughts, the more guilty you feel the more you think less of yourself. It's a complete attack on your character, personality and your faith! It is impossible to please God without Faith. Being stagnant and not fully embracing the gifts on the inside of me is not pleasing to God. If this sounds anything like your situation please use me as your sign to make the necessary adjustments now and put your faith into action so that you can hear God speak concerning your life. Stagnation is another tactic that the enemy loves to feed off of.

If you are so busy rehearsing your pain and walking in un-forgiveness that's enough to set your whole life backwards instead of forward. Be mindful that sometimes it's not what you go through, it's how you go through it. The lesson isn't a good lesson until you actually have proof you went through something. So why not do it with God, by Faith. You have nothing to lose but everything to gain when you trust the process with God. What does that look like? Remembering your Why! For life, family, business, and anything else that God calls you to do. Honoring God with your actions. People think God doesn't need them… Oh yes

He does! He needs a vessel to prove His Word through. He needs to be able to shine through His sons and daughters so that others will see what great things He has done through them. There is always somebody somewhere dealing with issues worse than yourself. BUT after a while, in God's timing He will cause you to shine bigger and brighter than you can imagine. "In due season you will reap if you faint not," Galatians 6:9

This is when things began to shift for me… Timing makes all the difference! My resting season was forming.

Fast forward to October 2023 I was definitely in a better place at this time. I began to feel this feeling of regret of retiring because I loved the gift God gave me so much. It kept tugging on me that I should return back to doing hair. I had pursued an opportunity that presented itself for me to professionally work in a space where I could service clients again. It worked for several weeks but then ended up not working out due to an unforeseen decision that had been made concerning this specific location. At the time I did question my decision of returning because I was expecting it to work out. However that same love and passion kept riding me, I wanted to come back to the hair industry really badly. So now at this time I decided to fast and pray. I kept talking to God about what I really wanted to do. I was very specific, very detailed even down to the type of clients I wanted to service. I told God I wanted to be able to specifically do haircuts as one of my specialties.

Fast Forward again to May 2024, I decided I'm officially returning back to the hair industry and this time I would pursue what I really want to specialize in. I wanted to specialize in healthy hair & short cuts.

Faith While Waiting

June 2024 I found the perfect spot for me to announce my return. One day while preparing and cleaning my new salon suite, I was praying and anointing my building. I prayed for the right clients, the aura of the environment, the type of clients I wanted & the heavenly experiences for both me & my clients. I envisioned how I would be able to share my wisdom and expertise with them. It was heavy in my spirit that I was needed! I remember one day while cleaning and bringing my supplies in, I was sweeping the floor, then I heard the Holy Spirit say, "This time it's going to be different because there are women waiting on you!" The excitement increased in my spirit even more. I remember feeling grateful, overjoyed like a release. It was a release like finally I know what it is I am supposed to be doing in this next season.

I went on a mission to journal the thoughts and ideas that were now being shown to me. I rebranded my site color scheme to reflect my new booking options and new look. I started advertising that I was officially back and started receiving bookings within my first week! For each client I have serviced they have allowed me to showcase my work via social media which has allowed me to showcase my master cuts. Every single day someone is booking one of my services. I am meeting my ideal customers and experiencing God's favor.

It has truly been an honor to share this story with you. If I had not put those boundaries up so that I could properly heal, if I hadn't embraced the reality that I needed to heal as well as grieve my Dad I may have still been in a stuck space, unable to hear God's plan for my life. I did not know I needed to experience this kind of love and passion for hair again. I did not know how much my clients needed a stylist like me to help them maintain their natural hair. This has literally come back around and has been such a beautiful experience. There have been clients sharing their testimonies with me about why they chose me and literally sharing that they have been looking for a stylist like me. It has been just like God said it would be!

If I could leave you with one thing it would be to believe God like your life depended on it. If you are in a place of waiting… Stay there until you receive your next set of instructions. God knows the plans He has for you. Jeremiah 29:11 NIV Make your requests known to Him in prayer with thanksgiving. That means pray about it with expectation to receive then rejoice about! If you've been in the waiting phase and feel like nothing is moving, ask yourself are you holding on to something that may be preventing you from receiving. Don't allow other people's opinion of you to make you doubt what God has already said about you. If you need to disconnect for a period of time then do that.

Most importantly, Be unapologetically you! Don't dim your light in order to make others feel comfortable. Some people are operating out of past hurt and that's all they know how to do. You are not alone and if you need to speak with someone one-on-one, then do that. I appreciate you taking the time to read my story and I pray all things remain well and prosperous for your life! Remember to pursue Faith over everything!

Lisa Freeman

Who is Lisa Freeman?... She calls herself "A Faith Girl" for it's by faith that she fought for herself, believed in herself, and won victories for herself!

She is a Serial Entrepreneur who began her professional career 29 years ago. She started braiding hair at the age of 13 and later pursued a professional career as a Cosmetologist in her hometown Richmond, VA. In 2002 she moved to Raleigh, NC where she has continued to build her entrepreneurial career.

Lisa is affectionately known as a person of inspiration, self-motivation, and style. Some of her hobbies include family time, DIY projects, shopping, reading, and studying personal development. When asked what's one thing you wished you would have done as a teenager? Her answer was, "I wish I wouldn't have wasted so much time wishing I "fit in" with my peers...I later found out it was preparing me to actually be the change!" When asked, If you could give one success nugget about your entrepreneurial journey what would it be? Her answer was, "To spend every day, several times a day telling yourself, "I can do all things through Christ who strengthens me!" Our words are powerful and using them to speak life over ourselves is the key.

Lisa has 3 adult children and 4 grandchildren. She is the owner and creative stylist of an online women's fashion boutique called "Looks by Lisa Freeman" She offers personal styling and she recreates designs. She's an author of her first book "Be the Change" and she has co-authored "Moments for Moms: Volume I and II

Together with her husband "Len" they lead with a life of faith, family, and fun. They have been married 29 years and together 33. They both are advocates in the wellness industry where they assist individuals with maintaining a healthier lifestyle. They also are the founders of a marriage platform called "Marriage That Works" where they provide practical and faith-based advice to couples desiring marriage or needing marital assistance.

Lisa also is the Founder of a women's community called "Let's Build Her Up". A platform for women of all ages, backgrounds, and ethnicities to be inspired to fulfill their purpose and passion in life.

Her life's mantra: *Live every day like it's a gift from God!*
You can connect and follow her movement through her website.

Contact Information:

Website: www.looksbylisafreeman.com
Email: hello@looksbylisafreeman.com
Facebook: Lisa Freeman
Instagram: thisis_lisafreeman
TikTok: Looksbylisafreeman

"When you are waiting, God is preparing you for something greater than you can imagine."

– Anonymous

Chapter Three

Crystal D. Harrison
"The Faith to Wait"

"Trust in the Lord with all your heart and lean not on your own understanding; in all your ways submit to him, and he will make your paths straight."

-Proverbs 3:5-6

In the quiet moments of life, amidst the noise of daily routines, there lies a profound longing within each of us: the desire to understand our purpose and where it will lead us. This quest for meaning can often feel uncomfortable, and yes even scary especially when the answers seem to elude us. As I navigate through my own personal journey of "Faith While Waiting", I have found myself often in a season of waiting, and yearning for clarity on the purpose God has destined for me along this journey called life.

It is vitally important that we choose to embrace our own personal journey ahead. While we may not have all the answers, remember the assurance of God's presence and purpose. The ultimate revelation is not just about the destination but about the deepening of our relationship with Him. In waiting, we must discover that purpose is not a destination to reach but a path to walk, illuminated by faith, hope, and love.

I have felt the burden of waiting in expectation and trust me it is rarely comfortable. My waiting season has been filled with questions that I ask myself: Am I doing enough? Is this the right path? What if I never find out? The weight of expectation can feel heavy, even in my life at various times feeling a pressing down on my heart. Yet, within this burden lies an opportunity for growth both spiritual and emotional. I'm reminded of Proverbs 3:5-6: *"Trust in the Lord with all your heart and lean not on your own understanding; in all your ways submit to him, and he will make your paths straight."* These words echo in my mind, urging me to relinquish control and embrace the uncertainty of what is ahead, because I trust God even in my waiting season.

I am embracing my journey as I wait, It was necessary to begin to see that the journey itself holds value. In this season, I discovered the beauty of patience. Patience is not merely about passively biding my time; I am in an active pursuit of God through prayer, meditation, and scripture. Isaiah 40:31: *"But those who hope in the Lord will renew their strength..."* Each day I spend seeking Him transforms my waiting into a dynamic experience, allowing me to spiritually grow in faith and resilience as God draws me closer to Him.

Listening for the whisper In moments of solitude are simply life changing, I have learned to listen for God's gentle whisper. I remember a time when the impatient Crystal tried to figure it out between moments of wanting and waiting. Having an understanding of the waiting stage has compelled me to quiet my own thoughts and open my heart to God's whisper. Psalm 46:10 invites me to *"Be still, and know that I am God."* It is in these still moments that I feel His presence most profoundly. I start to understand that my purpose may not be a grand revelation but rather a series of small nudges guiding me along the way. Waiting and listening to the very heartbeat of God after experiencing unimaginable sorrow twice within a year and a half has taken on a new meaning for me. The moments stretch and blend into an eternity of heartache, and yet, in that stillness, there emerges a whisper—a heartbeat that echoes through my pain. This is my journey of waiting and listening to the heartbeat of God during one of the most challenging seasons of my life, a season marked by the tragic loss of our sons, Mekhi James and Micah Timothy Harrison.

On January 25, 2023, my world shattered when Mekhi was taken from us. A life full of promise, cut short by an act of gun violence. In that instant when my daughter Romesha called to ask the question: Why is RIP on Mekhi's Instagram page? Time stood still for me; because while I had no idea of the answer to this question something in my spirit quickened and I knew as I immediately rushed from work. The sounds of everyday life faded into silence, that would cause a feeling of a heavy weight of grief pressing down on my heart. Questions swirled: Why him? Why us? The loss was too profound to articulate, yet in the darkest moments, I felt a gentle prompting—*"Wait Crystal."*

This was not the answer I sought at the time. I craved understanding, resolution,, anything that would ease the pain of such a sudden and senseless loss. But as I sat in the reality of my grief, I began to sense something deeper beneath my sorrow—a heartbeat, steady and unwavering. In the silence, I turned up my prayer, allowing my brokenness to flow out to God.

There were days that I would listen for the comfort that followed Mekhi's passing, I sought comfort in the Word. Psalm 34:18 began to resonate with me at a deeper level: *"The Lord is close to the brokenhearted and saves those who are crushed in spirit."* In one of my most challenging seasons, I felt the presence of God almost like He was enveloping me, a reminder that even in my brokenness, I was not alone. I began to realize that waiting in this season was not about stagnation but rather about learning to lean into the divine comfort that only God could provide. As I waited, I learned to listen—not just for answers but for the gentle rhythm of God's heartbeat. It was a melody of love and compassion, woven through my pain. Each prayer became an act of surrender, allowing me to rest in the promise that God was still at work, even in my heartbreak.

Just when I began to navigate life without Mekhi, the unthinkable struck our family again. On May 19, 2024, our son Micah drowned in a tragic accident in Indiana at the Chinook FWA. The weight of grief doubled with reminders of losing my first twin, and I found myself in a chasm of despair so deep I could scarcely breathe at times. In those moments, the instruction to "wait Crystal" felt like a cruel joke from God. I questioned why must we endure this pain again? How much waiting could my heart bear? Yet, in the midst of my sorrow, I heard that same whisper that I heard when my marriage was under attack, and our son Mekhi was killed: *"Wait."* Though my heart felt crushed beneath the weight of the loss of another son; twin, I chose to trust. I turned to God with every ounce of my being, praying for strength and clarity in the midst of chaos and death. It was then that I began to understand that my waiting was not a sign of abandonment but an invitation to deepen my relationship with God—a chance to experience His heartbeat amidst the turmoil that was occurring in our lives.

As I continued to wait I found strength in the wait, and strength within my inner circle. Friends and family; and our spiritual parents surrounded us, offering love and support. Their presence became a tangible reminder of God's faithfulness. I remembered Ecclesiastes 3:1: *"There is a time for everything, and a season for every activity under the heavens."* I clung to the hope that this season of waiting was preparing me for something greater, even if I couldn't see it yet; and honestly there were times that I did not, but I trusted God. I trusted God!

In those long, quiet nights, I would sit with my grief and listen. I was reminded that waiting is not merely an absence of movement but an active engagement with God. I journaled my thoughts, pouring out my heart and allowing the Father to speak back to me through His Word. Every verse became a lifeline, each promise a reminder of His unfailing love specifically to me.

In the stillness, I began to perceive the heartbeat of God in a new light. His rhythm was one of compassion, understanding, and unwavering love. I realized that my grief was not a barrier but a pathway to a deeper intimacy between God and me. As I navigated my pain, I felt a sense of purpose emerging—an understanding that my journey could be a source of hope for others facing similar heartache. As I listened to God's heartbeat, I found peace in the midst of the chaos. The promise of Isaiah 41:10 became my anchor: *"Do not fear, for I am with you; do not be dismayed, for I am your God. I will strengthen you and help you; I will uphold you with my righteous right hand."* I understood that waiting was not a void but a space filled with divine presence, where healing could begin.

In this chapter of "Faith While Waiting", I learned that though my heart was heavy with loss, it is also filled with hope. As I listen to the heartbeat of God, I found the strength to carry my grief and share it with the world. My sons, Mekhi and Micah, may no longer walk beside me, but their legacy lives on in my heart. Waiting has transformed from a burden into a journey of trust, love, and a deeper understanding of God's infinite compassion. Though the road ahead can be uncertain, I am comforted by the knowledge that I am never alone. I choose to wait, not in despair but in hope, listening for the heartbeat of God that assures me He is with me in every moment of my life.

Waiting can be a profound experience, often filled with anticipation, hope, and sometimes frustration. Waiting is an act of faith and trust in God's perfect timing.

1. Trust in God's Timing

- **Scripture**: *"For I know the plans I have for you," declares the Lord, "plans to prosper you and not to harm you, plans to give you hope and a future."* (Jeremiah 29:11)
- God has a purpose for our waiting. Trusting in His plans can provide comfort as we navigate periods of uncertainty.

2. Strength in Waiting

- **Scripture**: *"But those who hope in the Lord will renew their strength. They will soar on wings like eagles; they will run and not grow weary, they will walk and not be faint."* (Isaiah 40:31)
- Waiting is not passive; it can be a time for renewal and growth. Relying on God during these moments can lead to inner strength and resilience.

3. Patience and Perseverance

- **Scripture**: *"Be still before the Lord and wait patiently for him; do not fret when people succeed in their ways, when they carry out their wicked schemes."* (Psalm 37:7)

- Patience is a key aspect of waiting. This verse encourages us to focus on our relationship with God rather than comparing ourselves to others.

Each passing day reinforces the vital lesson of trusting the process: waiting is part of that process. Just as seeds take time to grow beneath the soil, so does God's plan for our life. The cultivation of our purpose may not happen overnight, but we must trust that God is working in the hidden places. Romans 8:28 reassures me: *"And we know that in all things God works for the good of those who love him, who have been called according to his purpose."* This promise will fuel our hope, reminding us that every moment spent waiting is a step closer to fulfillment.

Crystal D. Harrison M.Ed.

Crystal Denise Harrison is truly a woman after God's own heart. She strives to "Raise the Standards" one opportunity, one woman and one purpose at a time in her pursuit to guide other women to discover their purpose and destiny in the Father. Crystal currently resides in Chester, Pennsylvania with her husband Jay of thirty-eight years. Crystal and Jay have seven children ranging in age from thirty-six years old to the youngest who is nineteen years old. Crystal and Jay are the proud grandparents to eight little ones.

Crystal is a graduate of Hampton University where she earned her bachelor's degree in Liberal Arts with a concentration in the ECE field. Crystal continued her education at the University of Phoenix earning a Master Degree in Early Childhood Education.

Crystal is a very involved community leader, mentor, and lifelong educator. Crystal has worked in the ECE profession for more than thirty years. She continues to provide ongoing support and guidance to other ECE professionals and Early Childcare organizations through Circle of Educators and CDH ECE Educational Resources and Services.

Crystal is the founder of CDH Ministries and Heart 2 Heart. Heart 2 Heart provides an opportunity to restore the hearts of women one opportunity at a time through mentoring, fellowship, and teaching, so that women can truly experience the love of God's purpose moving in their lives as He created and intended for us to live. Crystal believes that her desire to allow God to use her compassion and purpose in the lives of others will be a guide to many along their journey.

Crystal wrote her first book "How to Fight Fair in Marriage" in 2018 after her marriage was tested and tried. As other tests in her life she fought and won in "in the Ring of Marriage." Her second book "The Traits of Women of Grace" was released in 2023 is a collection of chapters Co-Authored by women who have made a significant deposit in her life over the span of thirty-plus years. "How to Fight Fair in Marriage" and "Traits of Women of Grace" may be purchased on Amazon.

Contact Information:
Email: 4cdhministries@gmail.com
Website: www.CDHMinistries.com
Facebook: Crystal Denise Harrison
Heart 2 Heart
Circle of Educators

"Be still before the Lord and wait patiently for him; do not fret when people succeed in their ways, when they carry out their wicked schemes."

– *Psalm 37:7*

Chapter Four

Marvastine Nichols

My Anchored Faith in God

"Trust in the Lord with all your heart. And lean not on your understanding; in all ways acknowledge to him, and he will make your paths straight."
-Proverbs 3:5-6 NIV

Faith while waiting is a powerful journey—one that proves the strength of those who trust God in every season, no matter how challenging. Those who have been through the storms of life know that God is always present, guiding us even when we can't see the way. God's goodness doesn't waver, even when life seems uncertain. It is during these seasons of waiting that our faith truly gets tested, refined, and strengthened.

I remember vividly the days I spent traveling with my children, making trips back and forth to visit family. I hoped to reach the next town each time, looking for a safe place to rest. There were moments I can barely explain because it was only God's grace that carried us. At that time, my job hours had been reduced, and the little overtime I relied on was gone. I prayed constantly, knowing my mother was eager to see us.

Like so many, I prayed for travel mercies—protection over the journey ahead. We would leave early in the morning to make the most of the daylight hours. When the road became long, and my eyes heavy with fatigue, I would stop at the nearest gas station to rest and stretch. My children, still small, would accompany me everywhere, as I kept a close watch for their safety. As a young mother traveling alone, I had to be cautious. I kept only a small amount of money easily accessible and the rest hidden, just in case.

Though I'm not a coffee drinker, snacks were my go-to to keep alert. I learned to stop only in well-lit areas and pushed forward, even if fatigue crept in. Driving at night, especially during the fall, was a challenge—the darkness always seemed heavier. I would blink and suddenly realize I had driven miles without remembering it. In those moments, I knew God was my co-pilot, holding the wheel when I couldn't. Time and again, I would make it safely, feeling His presence surrounding us as a protective shield.

I faced moments that tested my faith. There were times when the enemy tried to discourage me, playing tricks with my mind and filling my heart with doubt. But I stood firm on God's promises. His Word became my anchor, my shield against the storms of doubt. Even when I didn't see a way forward, I trusted that God was leading me. My faith carried me through loss, disappointment, and uncertainty. When others failed, God remained faithful. When life's challenges seemed overwhelming, He provided peace, comfort, and strength.

I've come to understand that God is faithful in every season—good or bad. He has been a Father to the fatherless, a friend who never abandons. My mother used to tell me that Jesus was the only friend I could completely trust, and I've found that to be true. Friends and family might disappoint, but God never does. He is always available to hear our fears, our worries, and our pain. He is the friend who never leaves and the Father who never fails.

God continues to work on me, revealing His plans and preparing me for new seasons. I know I haven't come this far to be silent or stagnant.

Even when I falter due to fear, laziness, or procrastination, God's grace is there to guide me back. I've realized that my faith during waiting seasons is not about what I can see, but about trusting what I cannot see—trusting God's timing instead of my own.

It's easy to ask God to move mountains for us, but we must also be willing to step forward in faith. Have we done our part? Are we truly living out the faith we profess, or do we just expect God to make it all happen without any effort on our end? It's a question we must all answer. God is the Alpha and Omega, the beginning and the end, and there is no other like Him. We are called to praise and thank Him, even while waiting, knowing that His timing is perfect.

When I surrender my worries to God, I find peace in the waiting. I trust that whatever I'm praying for will come in God's time. And if it doesn't, it's because He has something better in store. The enemy may try to sow doubt, but I choose to keep my eyes on Christ, confident that He is fighting on my behalf.

Practical Tips for Strengthening Your Faith While Waiting
1. **Pray Continually**
   Develop a habit of prayer, not just in moments of crisis but as a daily practice. Start each day by thanking God and laying your concerns before Him. Keep a prayer journal to track your prayers and how God answers them.
2. **Stay Rooted in God's Word**
   Spend time reading and meditating on scripture. Find verses that speak to your current season and memorize them. Let God's Word be your comfort and strength in times of waiting.

3. **Surround Yourself with Encouragement**
   Connect with a community of faith, whether it's a small group, church, or online fellowship. Surround yourself with people who will encourage you, pray with you, and speak life over your situation.

Marvastine Nichols

Marvastine Nichols graduated from the University of Arkansas at Monticello - CTM in 2011 with an Associate of Applied Science, focusing on Early Childhood Education. She obtained her Associate of Arts degree from the University of Arkansas at Monticello in 2016. She plans to complete her Bachelor of Applied Science degree in the upcoming spring..

She worked for many years as a substitute teacher, gaining valuable experience in the public school system. Marvastine has a credible background in education, having served as a Head Start Lead Teacher for five years.

Additionally, as a committed servant to her community, she served for two years as an AmeriCorps Digital Divide Worker. She has always loved working in her community and with the youth. She organized her first community Black History Program as a volunteer AmeriCorps Digital Divide Worker with the help of school staff and youth.

Her literary accomplishments are notable. Her debut self-published book, Pursuing Purpose in the Midst of it All, has inspired countless readers. Her upcoming co-authored book, Faith While Waiting, is eagerly anticipated and set to be released soon.

She has been a featured author in Making the Headline News and Author's Impact Hub Spotlight, as well as a featured guest on the Author's Impact Hub Podcast.

Contact Information:

Instagram: @MarvastineNichols
Facebook: Marvastine Nichols
Website: www.AuthorMarvastineNichols.com

"In the waiting, God is working."

– Anonymous

Chapter Five

Josias Jean-Pierre

Hold up!! Hold on!!

[20] Now to him who is able to do immeasurably more than all we ask or imagine, according to his power that is at work within us, [21] to him be glory in the church and in Christ Jesus throughout all generations, for ever and ever! Amen.
-Ephesians 3:20-21

Oftentimes we can lose hope because of what can't be seen. Sometimes, we may even ask ourselves what is the purpose of holding on when how it looks, looks like is getting worse? Why am I in this? What did I do to deserve this? These are common questions that we may have when the storm that was out of your control came onto your lap. It's easy to tell others to not give up and to hold onto their faith when you're not in the midst of anything. Sometimes we may find ourselves struggling to believe the very thing we tell other people when we face our own mess in life. We can be so good at singing praise and worship but when the storms come in life, do we still praise in the midst of it? Do we still worship in the midst of it? Or do we allow the storm cause us to believe that God is not able to do exceedingly, abundantly, above all that we can ask for or imagine? (Ephesians 3:20-21) Do we allow the storm that hits make us forget that if God can do it before, He can do it again?

Having faith while waiting is a very hard thing to do especially when you're in the 'I need it right now' season. When you're in the season where it feels like waiting can no longer be an option. I was in that season of saying forget waiting and forget trying to activate faith when it seems like nothing is coming through for me. I was getting to a point in life where I did not feel like there was hope or purpose for me in this world even though I saw a vision of platforms I was going to be on at a young age. When the pain of life is hitting you left and right it's hard to keep on activating your faith and wait when healing is what you need right now. I was hanging onto a thread but in need of a lifeline because I had no more energy to keep on going and to keep faking it hoping that I will make it. I was trying to run this race of life with my own understanding, my own strength, and my own will and getting mad at God for the outcome when he wasn't even thought of in the process. I was in this battle of my life that made me question my existence and because of that, I attempted suicide three times believing I was not fit.

At a young age of five years old, my father looked at my brothers and I in the eye and told us, "never call me dad, I am not your dad, call me pastor." I grew up believing this man was not my dad and from the age of five I always called this man pastor. I was diagnosed with epilepsy as a child and had to go to the hospital for the first 13 years of my life as if the hospital was my second home. Fell into a category of special education, had an IEP (Individualized education plan) was told by peers and educators to throw in the towel and give up because my hopes and dreams will never come through. Then having to deal with a father wound and not having the right representation. I was yearning for a fathers love and fathers guidance, yearning for a miracle and a breakthrough. Yearning to hear the words of affirmations from my father. This was a pain of mine that I could never process through. I was tired of battling the fight of epilepsy and tired of feeling the neglect, pain, rejection, abandonment, from my father. It was hard to see God as the father when I grew up believing I was fatherless. It was hard to believe that God is the father to the fatherless when my own biological father who is a pastor said to never call him dad.

Even though I felt those things, there was something in me that was pulling me closer to God. No matter how many times I let go of Him, He never let go of me. I remember opening the Word one day and I read the book of Hebrew chapter 13 verse 5, "keep your lives free from the love of money and be content with what you have, because God has said, never will I leave you nor forsake you." I remember reading that passage and there was a hover that came over me. I then flipped my Bible to a random chapter and I opened Psalm 68:5 and it said, "A father to the fatherless, a defender of widows, is God in his holy dwelling" I remember reading both passages and I felt a peace that surpassed all understanding. I sat down and told God, "look I am tired of waiting and feeling what I am feeling, tired of this pain. I am trying to win this but I can't." This is where the shift for me began. God led me to read Ephesians 6:12-17 it says, " [12] For our struggle is not against flesh and blood, but against the rulers, against the authorities, against the powers of this dark world and against the spiritual forces of evil in the heavenly realms. [13] Therefore put on the full armor of God, so that when the day of evil comes, you may be able to stand your ground, and after you have done everything, to stand. [14] Stand firm then, with the belt of truth buckled around your waist, with the breastplate of righteousness in place, [15] and with your feet fitted with the readiness that comes from the gospel of peace. [16] In addition to all this, take up the shield of faith, with which you can extinguish all the flaming arrows of the evil one. [17] Take the helmet of salvation and the sword of the Spirit, which is the word of God."

I chose to wait and put on God armor and because I put on his armor, I am epilepsy free, I was able to forgive the father wound, heal from depression and suicidal thoughts. I now walk in my full purpose and go down the elevator to help others be equipped so they can flourish and elevate fully into whom God created them to be. There's a message in the wait because while you're in the wait, it's building things inside of you that shapes character development. It also created a message that can be transformational for someone else. God used what I thought was ugly and made it beautiful. Turned my mess into messages, test into testimonies and miseries into ministries.

The faith acronym I created stands for: fully activate in the heavens. We need to understand that in order to bring heaven to earth, our faith needs to be fully activated in the heavens if we want God to do something in the earth. He's a God that can move mountains but in order for the mountains to move, we need faith to be in the driver's seat. Hebrews 11:6 says, But without faith it is impossible to please him: for he that cometh to God must believe that he is, and that he is a rewarder of them that diligently seek him."

Practical Tips to Help Activate Your Faith

1. Focus on God's Promises
Keep your faith *Fully Activated In The Heavens* by reminding yourself of God's promises. Memorize and meditate on scriptures that encourage you, like Hebrews 11:6 or Ephesians 6:12-17. Write them down and place them where you can see them daily—whether on your mirror, refrigerator, or phone background—to keep your focus on God's truth rather than your circumstances.

2. Actively Trust Through Prayer

Fully activating your faith means leaning into prayer even when it's hard. Set aside time each day to pray specifically for the areas where you're struggling. Use the Bible as a guide for your prayers, turning promises into declarations over your life. Trust that God is working behind the scenes, even when you can't see it, and allow your faith to shift your perspective from earthly limitations to heavenly possibilities.

3. Take Faith-Filled Actions

Faith isn't just about believing; it's about taking steps that align with that belief. Identify one small, faith-filled action you can take today, even if it's as simple as forgiving someone, serving others, or pursuing a goal that feels beyond reach. By taking these small steps, you're allowing your faith to be the driver, trusting that God will handle the outcome in His perfect timing

Faith While Waiting

Dr. Josias Jean-Pierre

Josias Jean-Pierre is a renowned motivational speaker and an award winning national and international author. He is a 7X author and Amazon number one best seller. His mission and vision is to help others be equipped with the tools that they need so they can be empowered and elevate fully into whom God created them to be. His impact in the world has reached the eyes of major media outlets such as, Forbes, Forbes One where he was recognized as one of the top authors to look out for in 2024, Forbes 30 under 30, Los Angeles Wire, Los Angeles 30 under 30 with Ariana Grandè & Lil Nas X, Thisis50 with the G unit brand, The American Reporter, CEO Weekly, New York Weekly, Yahoo finance where he was featured with Ice Cube as one of the top 10 inspirational African Americans of 2021, Sheen Magazine, Vision and purpose Magazine, Our Blk Men Magazine, Heart Of Hollywood Magazine, We Empower Magazine, Voice of change magazine where he was featured as one of the top 30 transformational entrepreneurs making global impact. He is a nominee for an honorary doctorate out of Trinity International Ambassadors University and a three-time presidential lifetime achievement award recipient of 2024.

Contact information:

Email: Josiasjeanpierre@gmail.com
Instagram: @Coachwith_Josias

"Wait for the Lord; be strong and take heart and wait for the Lord."
– Psalm 27:14

Chapter Six

Verenda K. Cobbs

Building Faith After Grief and Loss

The LORD is my shepherd He restoreth my soul: he leadeth me in the paths of righteousness for his name's sake. Yea, though I walk through the valley of the shadow of death, I will fear no evil: for thou art with me; thy rod and thy staff they comfort me.

-Psalm 23:1,3-4

When I say the word FAITH...I have to share with you that some of my most powerful memories of faith come from spending New Year's Eve with my grandmother after the holidays. She had a tradition of making sure that everyone in the house was on their knees, praying as the new year arrived. I can still picture her on her knees in the living room, sometimes with tears in her eyes, faithfully connecting with God in those moments. As I grew older, I asked her about her prayer life, and she shared so much wisdom with me. She talked about how she learned to walk with God, to pray consistently, and to trust Him through everything life threw at her. She spoke about how God provided for her and her children and how she leaned on her faith no matter what happened. My grandmother became a pillar of faith and resilience in my life. Through her, I learned what it truly meant to have a deep, unwavering faith in God, and she instilled in me the value of resilience through her example.

My grandmother passed away in 2018, and since then, one of my greatest challenges has been holding onto my faith in God while trying to walk in the fullness of my purpose. Her loss left me feeling lost, depressed, and discouraged—not only in ministry but also in pursuing the dreams I had once been so passionate about. It felt as if the very foundation of my faith had been shaken, and I often questioned whether I had any real faith. Her loss impacted me deeply because I found myself waiting on God with a heart weighed down by grief and doubt. This journey has tested me time and time again and has been one of the hardest things I've ever faced. I wrestled with deep feelings of abandonment, wondering why God would allow such profound pain. The promises He had spoken over my life seemed distant, overshadowed by the weight of my hurt.

But through it all, I came to understand that faith isn't just about believing when everything is going well; it's about trusting Him when the path ahead is unclear and the future feels uncertain. This journey of walking through grief and doubt has been one of the greatest challenges of my life, but it has also led to some of my most significant personal growth. It taught me that true faith is forged in those moments when we have to rely on God, even when we don't understand the "WHY" Why and WHAT became my biggest questions! Why did this happen now? What am I going to do without my role model?

When my grandmother passed away, I went through several different emotions including all of the stages of grief that they describe traditionally. During the summer of 2018 into the fall, I went through a range of emotions that mirrored the stages of grief, though not in a linear way. The shock of her passing hit me first—it felt surreal like I was in a fog. I couldn't fully comprehend that someone who had always been a pillar in my life was gone. Next, I experienced denial. I threw myself into work and daily routines to distract myself from facing the reality of her loss. It was my way of protecting myself from the pain, convincing myself that I could manage without fully dealing with my emotions. Then came anger. I felt frustrated and even angry with God for allowing this loss to happen. I questioned His plan and struggled to understand why someone so dear to me had to be taken away. My faith, which had once been my foundation, felt unstable as I wrestled with my emotions. During this time, I was also struggling to process what I wanted to do with ministry and life. I went to work daily and still found myself feeling like something was missing in my life. Bargaining followed as I found myself reflecting on things I could have done differently—spending more time with her, being more present, and cherishing the moments we had together. I asked myself if I could have prayed harder for her healing or been a better granddaughter in some way. These thoughts consumed me as I longed for one more moment with her.

Depression set in next, and this was perhaps the hardest stage. I felt utterly lost and overwhelmed. My passion for ministry and life itself diminished. I found it hard to get up each day and push forward because the grief seemed too heavy to carry. Everything felt meaningless, and I struggled with feelings of hopelessness. It was at this stage that I questioned whether I had the strength to continue pursuing my purpose, as it seemed distant and out of reach. Finally, I began to find acceptance, though it didn't come easily. I realized that grief doesn't mean I have to forget her or the pain of losing her, but that I can honor her memory while moving forward in my life. Acceptance for me didn't mean the absence of pain, but learning to live with it while still choosing to trust God's plan for my life. My faith became more resilient as I leaned on Him for comfort and understanding, knowing that my grandmother's legacy lives on through the way I walk in my purpose.

Between November 2018 and December 2018, I found myself in a pivotal moment of my life. In the aftermath of my grandmother's passing, I turned to journaling as a way to process my emotions and make sense of the losses I was experiencing. Writing became my outlet, a space where I could express my grief, frustration, and uncertainty about the future. The weight of my loss had not only shaken my faith but also drained my will to continue in ministry. I felt lost, disconnected from my purpose, and unsure about where God was leading me.

However, everything changed when I attended the "Woman Thou Art Loosed" conference in Texas. That weekend marked a turning point in my journey. During the conference, I had a life-altering encounter with God. It was here that I received a renewed sense of purpose and clarity. God began to reveal to me His plan for my life, specifically around the themes of resilience, faith, and overcoming trauma. It was during this time that I received the name for my ministry and business and felt the call to become a published author. The insight and revelation I gained that weekend breathed new life into me, reminding me that I was called to serve, despite the pain I had experienced.

By December 2018, I had self-published my first book, marking the beginning of a new chapter. This step was a significant leap of faith, but it laid the foundation for what was to come. Since then, I've participated in several anthology projects and written devotionals, workbooks, and other books. What started as a season of loss and uncertainty turned into a journey of rediscovery and purpose.

The journey wasn't without its challenges. The obstacles I faced during this time were numerous, and perhaps the most overwhelming of all was the fear of failure. Doubt became a constant companion as I questioned whether I was truly capable of fulfilling the calling God had placed on my life. Fear gripped me—fear that I wouldn't measure up, that my efforts would fall short, and that I might fail not only myself but those who depended on me.

Emotionally, I battled frustration, anger, and sadness, feeling weighed down by the immense grief of losing my grandmother. On top of that, the loss of my best friend Halona and my godmother compounded my feelings of heartache and anxiety. There were days when I questioned whether I had the strength to continue, and I often felt overwhelmed by the emotional toll these losses took on my heart and spirit.

Amid the grief, fear, and uncertainty, I relied heavily on a variety of coping mechanisms that helped me to navigate through these difficult emotions. One of the most powerful tools for me was prayer. Prayer became my lifeline, my way of staying connected to God even when I didn't have the answers. Meditation also helped me to find moments of peace and stillness, allowing me to center myself and find clarity.

I sought out counseling, both group and individual, which provided me with a safe space to process my grief and explore my emotions more deeply. Life coaching and mentorship were also vital, offering guidance and support as I stepped into my calling. I found strength in my community, especially in the support of my mom, aunt, uncle, and close friends. Their presence reminded me that I wasn't walking this journey alone.

Community support became a huge part of my healing process, as I leaned on others who could empathize with my experiences. Group support, whether through ministry or other circles, helped me feel connected and reminded me of the power of shared healing. Through these practices—prayer, counseling, meditation, and the love of my community—I was able to regain my footing and continue pursuing the purpose God had set before me.3. Faith Journey

My faith was deeply tested as I entered the launch phase of my ministry between 2022 and 2023. The fear of failure loomed large, especially as I reflected on the closing of my church back in 2018—a moment that left a significant mark on my life. That experience had shaken my confidence, and I questioned whether I had the strength to rebuild and step back into the calling God had placed on my life.

Women's empowerment came naturally to me, and I could focus on that with ease, but launching a ministry again felt daunting. Doubt crept in, whispering that I might not succeed or that I wasn't ready. I found myself dragging my feet, procrastinating, and holding back, even when God was clearly telling me to move forward. I came up with excuses—telling myself that the timing wasn't right, that I wasn't equipped, or that I needed more preparation. But in reality, I was afraid.

Still, God's voice persisted. Despite my hesitation, I started with what I could. I launched a podcast, using my platform to inspire and speak to those who needed encouragement. Then I moved into teaching courses online via Zoom, reaching people in ways I never thought possible. I started a support group for women, creating a space where we could come together and heal. Eventually, I stepped out in faith and began a prayer call, and that led to in-person services and conferences. Each step forward was a reminder that God was guiding me, even when my faith wavered.

Throughout this journey, certain scriptures, quotes, and mentors became anchors for my faith. Romans 8:28, which reminds me that all things work together for the good of those who love God, was a source of hope during times of uncertainty. Psalm 40 spoke to the waiting season, encouraging me to trust that God would lift me up in His perfect timing. These verses were constant reminders that God was with me, even when I couldn't see the full picture.

I was also blessed with mentors who played pivotal roles in strengthening my faith. My mom became one of my biggest inspirations of faith as I navigated this hard place in my life. I moved back home in 2018 and as I look back, I remember her praying for me, encouraging me, and pushing me to not to give up. Even during some of my darkest moments, she reminded me that there was still more life to live and that I needed to keep going.

God also sent some amazing mentors into my life during the pandemic to encourage my journey of faith: Dr. Karen Lomax, Dr. Frances Bailey and Winifred Maddirala were voices of wisdom and guidance. My spiritual parents, Prophet Kia Simpkins and Apostle EJ Simpkins, were steady rocks, continually pushing me to trust God and step out in obedience. And, of course, my sisters and friends, who stood by me, encouraged me and held me accountable, were invaluable in this season of growth.

There were key moments along the way that solidified my faith and showed me just how faithful God truly is. Traveling out of the country for the first time opened my eyes to the global impact God was calling me to have. It was a revelation that I was meant for more than I had ever imagined.

Attending Kingdom Faith Restoration Center also marked a pivotal shift in my life. I joined a church in 2023 and stepped into a place of support, love, and accountability after not being connected to a real church family for many years. It was there that I experienced the power of true leadership and spiritual covering, which reignited my passion for ministry. And being part of the Leadership Metro Richmond Class of 2022 was another game-changer. Through that experience, I learned how to harness my voice as a leader, developed a deeper understanding of resilience, and came to realize that giving up was no longer an option. Each of these moments reinforced my belief that God had been preparing me all along, and all I needed to do was step into my calling with faith and boldness.

This journey of waiting, trusting, and stepping out despite fear has shaped me into the leader I am today. What once seemed impossible became a reality as I allowed God to lead me, and in doing so, my faith has grown stronger than ever before.

My journey included navigating fear, hesitation, and ultimately surrendering to God's will to find resolution in ways I couldn't have imagined. I took the steps of faith necessary to publish several books, not only sharing my story but also creating resources that could empower others. I founded a community where people could build their faith and resilience together—a safe space for those who have faced adversity to share their stories and experiences. In doing so, I launched The Resilience Conference, an event that brings people together to find healing and hope. Additionally, The Queens Chronicles became a platform where I wrote about my journey of ministry and gave other women an opportunity to do the same. This experience was not just a project but a testimony of God's power to heal and restore.

Between 2018 and 2023, I grew in ways that I never anticipated. I learned the value of relationships—understanding that we are not meant to walk through life's challenges alone. I also realized the power of forgiving myself for the times I felt inadequate or had fallen short. Learning to forgive myself opened the door to deeper healing. Navigating adversity became less about the obstacles and more about how I responded to them. I grew stronger, learning that setbacks are not the end but simply stepping-stones toward my purpose. Most importantly, I developed resilience, recognizing that God had equipped me with the tools necessary to bounce back from life's most difficult moments.

I also learned how to embrace vulnerability. For so long, I believed I had to be strong all the time, but sharing my pain and struggles helped others as much as it helped me. This experience taught me that vulnerability is a strength, and it has allowed me to connect with others on a much deeper level.

This journey profoundly impacted my faith and reshaped my perspective on waiting. I realized that waiting isn't wasted time—it's preparation. Through this season, my faith deepened, and I learned that resilience is built in the waiting. The very act of trusting God when the path ahead is unclear strengthened my belief in His perfect timing. I no longer see delays or setbacks as signs of failure but as opportunities for growth and greater alignment with God's will. My faith is now rooted in the understanding that, no matter the outcome, God is faithful, and His plans are always better than what I could have imagined. The waiting season taught me patience, persistence, and a greater trust in God's process.

Faith While Waiting

If you are going through a season of waiting, know this—you are not alone. I know how hard it can be to trust God when it feels like everything around you is falling apart. But I want to remind you that God is still working, even in the silence. Don't give up. Keep GOING! The waiting is part of the journey, and God uses it to shape and strengthen you. I've been there, in moments of doubt and frustration, but I can testify that when you push through with faith, you will see God's hand in ways you never expected. Trust that He is doing something in you and for you, even when you can't see it yet. Keep going, because God's promises are still true, and He hasn't forgotten about you.

Here are some Practical Tips that have also worked for me:

1. **Pray Daily:** Make prayer your lifeline. In moments of waiting, pray for clarity, peace, and guidance. Philippians 4:6-7 reminds us, "Do not be anxious about anything, but in every situation, by prayer and petition, with thanksgiving, present your requests to God. And the peace of God, which transcends all understanding, will guard your hearts and your minds in Christ Jesus."

2. **Start Over as Often as You Need To:** Don't be afraid to hit the reset button. Life will bring setbacks, but that doesn't mean you've failed. Lamentations 3:22-23 says, "The steadfast love of the Lord never ceases; his mercies never come to an end; they are new every morning; great is your faithfulness." Every day is an opportunity for a fresh start.

3. **Don't Fear Accountability and Support:** Let others into your journey. Surround yourself with people who will uplift you, hold you accountable, and remind you of God's promises. Ecclesiastes 4:9-10 tells us, "Two are better than one, because they have a good return for their labor: If either of them falls down, one can help the other up." Accountability is a blessing, not a burden.

4. **Trust God to Lead You:** Even when the way forward seems unclear, trust that God is directing your steps. Proverbs 3:5-6 encourages us, "Trust in the Lord with all your heart and lean not on your own understanding; in all your ways submit to Him, and He will make your paths straight." He knows the way, even when you don't.

Waiting is hard, but through it all, God is faithful. You are being prepared for something greater. Keep believing, keep praying, and keep trusting. Your breakthrough is on the way. No matter what **KEEP GOING!**

Verenda K. Cobbs

**PREACHER | RESILIENCY LIFE COACH | MENTOR
AUTHOR | GLOBAL SPEAKER**

Apostle Verenda K. Cobbs, affectionately known as *"Pastor V"*, is a spiritual leader with a profound calling on her life. Born in Baltimore, Maryland, she discovered her passion for Christ during her college years at Virginia Commonwealth University (VCU) in Richmond, Virginia. Immersed in small groups, she delved into the study of God's word, prayer, and the power of the Holy Spirit.

Through divine revelation and a transformative encounter during a revival, Verenda received her calling to ministry. She has since been licensed as a minister, ordained as an Elder, and installed as a Pastor. With a heart for equipping others, she has founded ministries, trained outreach leaders, and empowered pastors and elders across the United States.

As an Apostolic visionary, Verenda connects effortlessly with audiences from all walks of life. Her extensive involvement in ministry, spanning various roles such as Associate Pastor, Executive Pastor, Youth Pastor, and Senior Pastor, has granted her a holistic understanding of the ministry's intricacies.

Verenda's qualifications extend beyond traditional ministry, as she holds professional social work, leadership, religious studies, and life coaching credentials. With over 20 years of experience in diverse industries, including education, grassroots organizing, mental health, and nonprofit leadership, she brings a wealth of knowledge and expertise to her role.

Driven by a deep desire to support individuals, families, and communities, Verenda specializes in helping people overcome trauma, build resilience, and develop coping skills. Her passion is to see others thrive and achieve spiritual maturity.

A celebrated author and visionary, Verenda founded Aarise Kingdom Ministries, including Aarise Kingdom Queens Fellowship, under the guidance of the Holy Spirit. Believing in the transformative power of God's glory, she champions the belief that everyone can "Arise and Shine" after experiencing trauma, regardless of their circumstances.

Apostle Verenda Cobbs carries the fire of God within her, leading with grace, faith, and a commitment to empowering others on their spiritual journeys. Apostle Verenda is covered by her spiritual covenant parents in ministry Apostle EJ & Prophet Kia Simpkins, Senior Pastors of Kingdom Faith Restoration Center.

Contact Information:

Instagram: @verendakcobbs
Facebook: Verenda K. Cobbs
Website: https://linktr.ee/verendakcobbs

"I wait for the Lord, my whole being waits, and in his word I put my hope."

*– **Psalm 130:5***

Chapter Seven

Demetria Williams

Faith Under Fire

"But they that wait upon the Lord shall renew their strength; they shall mount up with wings like eagles; they shall run, and not be weary; and they shall walk, and not faint"

-Isaiah 40:31

My son has been in jail for twelve years for a crime he didn't commit. Yet, my faith, my family's faith has remained unshaken. A testament to our resilience and hope. This season of waiting has unearthed a deep well of strength within me, a strength that is firmly rooted in my unyielding faith that God can do all things.

As I started to write about Faith while waiting, I overcame depression, suicide, and other attacks during that week. The temptations blew in over and over. I was missing my son, I felt like this situation should've been over, I felt let down by the justice system, I felt like I was doing too much between school and working, and I had so many other feelings. Also, I was trying to figure out when God would end this storm, and the more I tried, I got depressed, and thoughts of suicide formed. My mind whispered all the thoughts my 'Self' wanted to hear. Words like' give up,' 'you're the only one dealing with this,' or' this will never end.' However, It was one of the most painful and challenging weeks. But I was able to make it through by worshiping God, listening to my gospel station, constantly praying, and fighting back my need to know when God was going to put an end to the horrible ordeal. My Faith in God was the anchor that kept me afloat in the storm of emotions. My unwavering belief in God gave me the strength to keep going.

Maintaining a good attitude while waiting to see my son acquitted hasn't been easy. I still can't grasp the fact that my son has not been set free when all the evidence proves him innocent. I expected God to do things on my timing, which disappointed me when God didn't. I found myself angry many days. I felt betrayed, and sometimes, it felt like God didn't hear my prayers.

The emotional rollercoaster I have been on has gone from anger to betrayal to doubt. This was a journey I had never expected to take since I am a Christian. I read the Bible daily and talk to God in prayer regularly. In the back of my mind, Christians should always be strong, even if that means holding everything in. But each time I realized this was far from the truth, I stopped trying to be strong and acknowledged my weakness to God. This act of acknowledging my weakness was crucial in my journey, and I hope it helps you feel understood and accepted in your own struggles. However, I didn't lose my Faith. I just had mixed my expectations with my Faith, and when they were not met, it brought forth doubt, anger, and all the other emotions. When I told myself God's timetable was different from mine and accepted that truth, my peace was instantly restored.

Although I let go of my expectations and held on to the fact that God's timetable is different, it hasn't made the situation less painful, but I continue to keep my Faith in the midst of waiting. This journey of Faith and resilience has not been easy, but it has transformed my understanding of God's plan in ways I never thought possible. I have emerged from this journey not weakened but stronger and more resilient. This transformation and growth is a testament to the power of Faith and resilience in the face of adversity.

Constantly reading the bible, praying, relying on God, fasting, listening to gospel music, listening to sermons, and fighting back the need to know when the situation would end has been my coping mechanisms. Every day, I make sure to have the proper spiritual mindset required to wait well. It's not easy because I couldn't fathom what it meant to wait on God. I honestly didn't know what waiting on God looked like on a practical, everyday basis. I would pray and ask God what He wanted me to do. I felt the urge to do something; if I wasn't doing anything, I felt like I had failed my son. I fought against two popular questions I kept asking myself, "Does waiting on God mean doing nothing, and what should I not do while waiting on God." But through it all, my Faith in God remained unwavering, and this Faith sustained me during the most challenging times. To my surprise, on the night I was writing on a Sunday, a remarkable woman of Faith called me, someone I never knew. She informed me that one of the Facebook posts I shared about my son brought her out of the darkness. She said her son had been framed. I sit at my desk in front of my laptop while listening to my now friend(sister) telling me how I blessed her. Here I was, fighting back so much that I never knew this painful storm my son and I were in was helping others. As I lay down that night, God revealed that what I saw as a mess and thought was a mess was one great message of hope to others because of my Faith in Him.

This storm has tested my Faith in ways I never imagined. Also, unanswered prayers about the situation tested my Faith. When God was silent in the darkest time, I felt like He had left me, and sometimes I would get so angry and wouldn't pray, but God would use a stranger to ask me if I could pray for the individual to get me to pray and it worked every time. In addition, my Faith was tested on October 1, 2024, when I received a message from my son. He said, "Mom, I got the reply from the state about my motion, and all they wrote was, I can't prove it." That message was a slap in the face because all the facts were in black and white. I sat in my car between classes on break and messaged my son back on the GTL GettingOut prison app to ensure him that God was in control. Although I said those words, I felt we hit a stumbling block. Yet, I prayed and held onto the scripture Romans 8:28. Fortunately, my inspiration has been the gospel music artist, Hezekiah Walker. His song, 'More Than A Conqueror' has encouraged me on this tedious journey.

Moments of revelation have reinforced my Faith. One day, my son was lying on his prison bed, and as he looked up towards the ceiling, the words, "God got you, appeared. Another time, when my son dreamed of a lousy tornado, he said he was tossed to and from then thrown on the ground. He said God put in his heart that he was weathering the storm. When my son looked around, the tornado had destroyed everything but him. God also gave me revelations, which made my Faith stronger. Unfortunately, at the time of writing our story, we are still waiting and trusting in God. Our situation has not been resolved, but we have Faith while waiting. By the grace of God, my son and I have grown closer to the Lord. We have learned that Faith is not the absence of a storm but trusting God in a storm.

Having Faith in God doesn't mean your emotions no longer exist. They do, and they flare up the most in moments of darkness. Just like they did for Elijah, the prophet, in the bible when Jezebel threatened to kill him. Elijah was afraid and fled for his life. He became so depressed that he prayed for death. He intentionally isolated himself in the wilderness. Elijah went from a mountaintop experience to defeating the prophets of Bal, but an episode of fear and failure followed the experience (1 Kings Chapter 19). Even though Elijah was afraid, he didn't lose his Faith. He had Faith; he prayed to die. It takes Faith to pray to God.

The first thing I constantly do is connect with my feelings like Elijah did. I'd love to say I always get this right, but I don't. My biggest struggle has always been avoiding my feelings because I always tried to be strong, but every time I did, I was weak and miserable.
Another thing I felt like, as a Christian, was that I shouldn't be afraid, angry, or any other emotions that we may feel when dealing with difficult situations. I always thought I should be strong when I have Faith in God, but God reminded me that having Faith in Him means acknowledging everything to Him. It doesn't make my Faith disappear or weak. It builds my Faith when I get in touch with my feelings and express to God what I am feeling, and He gives me the strength to process my emotions. God's strength is made perfect in my weakness. When we walk by Faith, battles attempt to set up camp in our hearts. But take heart: we serve a God more significant than anything we face in our lifetime. Yet, there is a common misconception that God solves all our problems, filling our lives with only blessings and joy. If this were true, the Apostle Paul would not urge Christians to "rejoice in hope, be patient in tribulation, be constant in prayer" (Romans 12:12). For most of us, patience is a virtue that does not come naturally. To be patient in tribulation requires a special grace from God. In the Greek text, the verb for "be patient" means to be persistent, refuse to stop, persevere." It's about keeping the Faith, even when life feels gritty.

Finally, to maintain Faith in your waiting season, constantly seek the Lord through prayer, feeding your spirit with the word, fasting, surrounding yourself with other believers, and listening to worship music. Be mindful that through our suffering, our bodies continue to share in the death of Jesus so that the life of Jesus may also be seen in our bodies. Also, remember that Paul reminds us that through many tribulations, we must enter the kingdom of God" (Acts 14:22). Please understand that "waiting" doesn't mean sitting around doing nothing. It means to trust in God, anticipate, and hope for His guidance. Also, fixing our gaze on Him: His invisible and eternal qualities, character, and love.

1. **Acknowledge Your Feelings**

Allow yourself to feel the full range of emotions without judgment. Emotions are not a sign of weak faith, but rather an opportunity to bring your deepest fears, doubts, and frustrations to God. Like Elijah, express what you're feeling openly in prayer.

2. **Separate Expectations from Faith**

Understand that your expectations may not align with God's timing. Faith isn't about getting what you want when you want it; it's about trusting in God's plan, even when it doesn't match your own. Regularly remind yourself that God's timing is perfect.

3. **Create a Daily Spiritual Routine**

Establish consistent habits that feed your spirit: daily Bible reading, prayer, worship, and fasting. Listen to worship music or sermons to stay encouraged. Make it a priority to engage with God, even in moments of deep despair.

Demetria Williams

Demetria Williams, an author and an Amazon Best Seller, has a diverse portfolio of twenty-something books. Her books, available at Barnes& Noble and online at Walmart and other stores, cater to a broad audience, ensuring that her inspiring stories are accessible to all, including you. Whether you're a young adult seeking adventure, a parent looking for heartwarming tales, or a professional in need of inspiration, Demetria's books have something for everyone. Their availability on these diverse platforms has even led to their coverage in the newspaper. Demetria's success is not just in her sales but also in her recognition, as she is a reward-winning Author, having won Author of the Year. But Demetria's greatest reward is being a mother to her four loving children and grandmother to her loving granddaughter. She is a shining example of balancing work and family, as she manages her responsibilities as a Caterpillar employee while finding time to enjoy life with her family.

Contact Information:

Facebook: Demetria Deshand Williams
Website: www.demetriadwilliams.com
TikTok: @demetria450
Instagram: @touchby_demetria

"Faith doesn't make things easy; it makes them possible."
– Luke 1:37

Chapter Eight

Philomena Whitehead

Faith in the Wilderness Season

"Now faith is the substance of things hoped for, the evidence of things not seen."
— Hebrews 11:1 (NKJV)

Faith is trusting God even when you can't see the results right away. For the past ten years, I've been living this truth, often finding myself on the brink of giving up. Yet, I've learned to trust in God's faithfulness. Hebrews 11:1 reminds us that faith is about believing in the *now*—not someday, not eventually, but now. This has been my journey: holding onto the hope that God would fulfill His promises, even when I couldn't see how it was going to happen.

There were moments when I wanted to abandon the journey altogether, wishing I could just live a simple, ordinary life without the weight of responsibility. But God wouldn't let me. He has a purpose for my life—a calling that is too important to set aside. Every time I wanted to quit, I felt His gentle reminder: the assignment He has given me isn't just for my benefit but for the benefit of others as well. That reassurance has kept me moving forward, and each time, my faith grew a little stronger.

The waiting period has been long and full of challenges. There were times when I was so frustrated that I thought I had made a huge mistake. I felt lost, unsure of whether I was on the right path, surrounded by the right people, or even headed in the right direction. I faced obstacles with finances, resources, and finding clarity about my life's direction. But through it all, I was reminded of the promise in James 1: "Count it all joy when you fall into various trials, knowing that the testing of your faith produces patience." I held onto that truth, even when my patience was running thin.

To keep my faith alive during those difficult moments, I immersed myself in prayer, meditation on God's Word, and the support of faith-based communities. I encountered leaders—bishops, apostles, ministers, prophets, and evangelists—who encouraged and mentored me. They allowed me to witness their own walks of faith up close, showing me what it looked like to truly trust God. This access was a rare gift, one that strengthened my own faith and taught me the value of submission, humility, and letting go of offenses.

My faith journey has been marked by trials and errors. I've learned that God often allows us to go through challenging seasons to refine our faith. One pivotal moment happened during a vision I had in 2020. I was living in a small room, feeling lost and unsure. One night, I heard a knock in a dream, and when I opened the door, I saw a hand reaching out to me. A voice said, "Come." The path before me was gold, and the surroundings were pure white. I felt God's invitation to step out in faith, to trust Him completely.

The next day, a confirmation came through a conversation with my aunt in Georgia. She asked if I had seen a golden path. I was amazed—God had confirmed my vision through her, reassuring me that I was still hearing from Him. This encounter became a turning point, strengthening my faith and reminding me that God was with me in the wilderness.

Faith While Waiting

During this season, books like *Battlefield of the Mind* by Joyce Meyer and *Lily Grace* by Susie S. Mozell-Smith became lifelines. They challenged my thinking and taught me how to overcome the mental battles I was facing. The lessons I learned about mindset, faith, and God's promises have stayed with me. I've realized that the wilderness season was about growth—it was about preparing me for what God had in store.

As my mindset began to change, I saw God move swiftly in my life. The doubts that had lingered for so long began to fade. I learned that with God, there is no need for a "Plan B" or "Plan C." His Word is final, and He is faithful to fulfill His promises. Once I fully embraced this truth, things started to shift. My faith grew stronger, and I began to see God's hand in every aspect of my life.

Now, I can look back and see how the wilderness prepared me. It stripped away old mindsets and revealed areas where I needed to grow. God used people and circumstances to guide me out of that season, just as He had promised. I found myself surrounded by favor—new opportunities, new relationships, and a new outlook on life.

If you are in a wilderness season, here are some practical steps to keep your faith strong:

1. **Stay Connected to the Word**: Regularly meditate on Scripture, especially verses that speak to faith and perseverance. Let God's promises be a constant reminder of His faithfulness.

2. **Pray Consistently**: Keep an open line of communication with God. Share your doubts, frustrations, and hopes. Prayer is not just about asking for things but about building a relationship with the One who guides you.

3. **Surround Yourself with Encouragers**: Find a faith-based community where you can receive support, encouragement, and mentorship. The journey is easier when you're not walking it alone.

4. **Read Faith-Building Books**: Invest in reading materials that will strengthen your faith and challenge your mindset. Books like *Battlefield of the Mind* and other spiritual resources can help renew your perspective.

Faith While Waiting

Philomena Whitehead

Philomena Whitehead is a woman of resilience, passionate about her work and dedicated to being a blessing to others. She is an author of more than four books. Philomena is an elder transitioning into a new season of life. She regularly ministers in her community and to those she encounters. She works as a PCA and an illustrator's assistant. Residing in Newport News, VA, she is a devoted mother to three children and four grandchildren. She finds joy in her family and in friends who have become like family to her. In every aspect of life, she believes in starting small. She is a woman of great faith and believes in God, even when she can't see Him or feel Him. She has the heart of the Father's love. She loves God's people, and she also serve as an advocate for those who are unable to speak for themselves. She assists with the needs of individuals as a representative.

Philomena desires that many and especially woman will be healed, delivered, set free and made whole from reading her life stories of testimonials and lessons in her life journey. As God has delivered Philomena from her childhood traumas and adult traumas, He begins to enlighten her life with His Glory.

Hallelujah, Glory be to God.

Contact information:

Website: https://linktr.ee/RBHL_LLC

https://square.link/u/NwkxcOzI

Facebook: https://www.facebook.com/philomena.simpson

Instagram: www.instagram.com/psmena

True faith begins when you can trust God with unanswered questions."
– Anonymous

Chapter Nine
Jay T. Harrison, Sr.

When the Lights Went Out

"For we live by faith, not by sight."
(2 Corinthians 5:7)

It was early in the morning, December 13, 2013, as I lay in bed after a good night's sleep. The comfort of my dreams still lingered, but a strange heaviness pulled me back to reality. I called out to my wife Crys, *"Can you turn on the light switch in the bedroom?"* But instead of the familiar flicker of illumination, I was met with an oppressive darkness. *"What time is it?"* I shouted, my voice echoing against the walls. The room felt dense, almost suffocating, and I realized with a jolt that I couldn't see anything—not even my hands right in front of my face. Panic set in as it dawned on me: I had gone blind.

Silently, I felt my way to the bathroom, where I hoped to catch a glimpse of myself in the mirror and understand what was happening. Each step was a careful negotiation of the space around me, guided by touch and sound, but the darkness felt impenetrable. As I reached the bathroom and stood before the mirror, I was met with an emptiness that shook me to my core. I couldn't see my reflection; the mirror was just another dark void. It was like floating in space—there was nothing but silence and darkness.

A wave of realization crashed over me: *I am blind! I've lost my sight.* My heart raced as thoughts flooded my mind. *Lord, what am I going to do?* The weight of uncertainty pressed down on me. How would I carry out my assignment as the Senior Pastor of True Vine? How could I preach and lead the people you entrusted to my care? For a brief moment, I felt lost and yes, even a little afraid I must admit. *Now what do I do?*

The spirit of fear began to whisper discouragement, filling my mind with doubt and unbelief. *You can't see, so you can't read. You can't drive. You're no good for anything anymore.* But in the midst of the darkness, I remembered who I was and whose I was. *1 Corinthians 6:19 says, "Or do you not know that your body is the temple of the Holy Spirit, who lives in you and was given to you by God? You do not belong to yourself".* I took a deep breath and began to worship, calling forth the strength I knew was within me from the Father. Philippians 4:4 says, "Rejoice in the Lord always; again I will say, rejoice". 2 Timothy 1:7 *"For the Lord hath not given me the spirit of fear, but of love, power, and a sound mind". I*n that moment, I chose to walk by faith and not by sight. 2 Corinthians 5:7 I may have been engulfed in darkness, but I was not alone. God's presence wrapped around me like a warm blanket, reminding me that my worth was not tied to my ability to see. I began to reflect on my calling, the purpose that had fueled my passion for ministry long before this moment. My family, and the people I shepherded relied on more than just my physical vision; they needed my heart, my guidance, and my unwavering faith in God.

As I stood in that darkened bathroom, I felt a shift within me. The initial panic transformed into a quiet determination. I might have lost my sight, but I refused to let it define my worth or diminish my calling. I was still a leader, still a shepherd, still a vessel of God's love and purpose. The road ahead would be challenging, but I knew I could lean on the strength of my faith and the support of my wife, family, and my congregation.

With every ounce of resolve, I lifted my head high and whispered, *I will not be afraid. I will trust in the Lord with all my heart.* In that moment of surrender, I felt the darkness begin to lift—not in the physical sense, but in my spirit. I would navigate this new reality with grace and courage, confident that even in the dark, God would guide my way.

"Lord, I trust You!" I declared, my voice steady despite the tremors of uncertainty that still coursed through my body. *This has not caught You by surprise; You knew this would happen before the world began.* As the words flowed from my heart, I felt a surge of conviction. This darkness didn't change the calling or assignment You have placed on my life. *Lord, I still trust You!*

I remembered the scripture that had long been my anchor: *"Yea, though I walk through the valley of the shadow of death, I will fear no evil; for You are with me."* The familiar verses wrapped around me like a shield, reminding me that even in my deepest fear, I was not alone. It was in this moment that I sensed the Lord asking me, *"Do you trust Me Jay?"*

With my heart pounding, I replied, "Yes, Lord, I trust You." It was a simple affirmation, yet it carried the weight of my entire being. *I am your eyes, and I have not failed thee,* He responded gently, a whisper of reassurance amid the chaos. *I will show you great and mighty things that are yet to come. Do you trust Me son?*

"Yes, Lord, I trust You," I affirmed again, my spirit lifting with each repetition of that sacred phrase. I felt a connection to the divine purpose that has always driven me, a reminder that my journey was far from over.

Yet, I couldn't ignore the reality of my situation. Battling diabetes had taken its toll on my health, and being uninsured had only added to the burden of my situation. I had fought through countless challenges, but the loss of my sight felt like the heaviest blow. Just the day before, I had driven home after Sunday service, feeling the warmth of the sun on my face as I dropped off our musician, who lived in Vineland, New

Jersey. Now, waking up on that Monday morning, the darkness enveloped me like a heavy fog.

In that moment of despair, I felt a flicker of hope igniting within me. I realized that my circumstances, however bleak, did not define my future. The struggles I faced had forged resilience in me, teaching me the value of faith and community. I thought of my family, congregation, and of the lives I was called to touch, and how my journey—though challenging—could serve as a testament to God's unyielding love, faithfulness, and grace.

The Lord was inviting me into a deeper relationship, a partnership that would allow me to spiritually see beyond my physical limitations. I could already hear the familiar voices of my family, and church family, their encouragement lifting me like wings. Together, we would navigate this uncharted territory, bound by faith, love, commitment, and prayer.

As I settled into that realization, I sensed the heaviness of fear begin to lift. I felt God's presence enveloping me, a reminder that even in the darkest moments, there was a light within, waiting to be ignited. *"Lord, I trust You,"* I whispered again, this time with a newfound conviction.

With each breath, I committed to walking this journey, not just as a man who had lost his sight, but as a man who was learning to see in ways I have never imagined. And as I stepped into this new reality, I felt ready to embrace whatever lay ahead, assured that God was guiding me every step of the way.

The visit to the doctor's office was a blend of dread and hope. As I sat in the sterile room, the air was thick with anticipation, the doctor entered with a serious expression. *"I have good news and bad news,"* he began, pausing just long enough for my heart to race quickly. *"The bad news is… you're blind."* The words hung heavy in the air, a stark reality crashing down around me. I felt the weight of the world settle on

Faith While Waiting

my shoulders, a sinking feeling that threatened to pull me under. *"But the good news is,"* he continued, with a glimmer of hope in his eyes, *"I can perform surgery. I can't promise that you will see again or how well you will see Pastor, but I can fix the problem."* He explained that diabetes had detached my retina, leading me into this period of blindness. I listened intently, trying to absorb the information while my mind raced with thoughts of uncertainty.

Yet, here we go another layer of bad news unfolded as he mentioned the cost of the surgery—at least $11,000 or more. My heart sank further. Without insurance, I felt as though I was trapped in an unfortunate nightmare. But then, in an unexpected turn, the doctor added, *"Let's test your knowledge of the Bible. If you can name three blind people from Scripture, I'll do your surgery for free."* I took a deep breath, focusing my thoughts. *"Paul, Samson, Blind Bartimaeus,"* I blurted out, almost surprising myself with the quickness of my answers. *"You got it!"* he exclaimed, a smile breaking through the tension that was present in the room. I felt like a small victory had just occurred for me, a moment of connection amidst the overwhelming news.

Just when I thought I had faced the worst, another wave of grace washed over me. One of my leaders at the church worked for a local orthopedic doctor who had learned about my condition. As my leader shared the good work our church was doing in the community, he mentioned how my pastoral care had impacted so many lives. The doctor was moved by our mission and wanted to learn more about my vision.

When we met, he looked me in the eyes and said, *"God told me to look out for your brother."* He went on to share that he would cover the cost of my surgery. Tears filled my eyes as I felt God's love manifesting in a way I never expected.

Faith While Waiting

At the same time, my spiritual father, and spiritual mother, Bishop Stanley K. Smith, and Pastor Kim A. Davis organized a fundraising effort during a state gathering. Their dedication led to an incredible $10,000 being raised that very service. It was as if God was orchestrating every detail, proving that I was not alone in this fight.

As the day of surgery approached, I felt a mix of nerves and anticipation. On the day of the procedure, my brother in Christ Pastor Parris Baker drove all the way from Erie, PA, to be there for me and my wife. His presence was a source of comfort, grounding me in the midst of uncertainty in this new reality of blindness.

Just before the surgery began, the anesthesiologist entered the room. He looked at me and said, *"I hear you're a son of God? Can I pray for you?"* His request caught me off guard, but I nodded eagerly. He prayed fervently, and as he did, I felt the presence of God fill the room, a warm embrace that calmed my spirit.

When I woke up, I found myself speaking in tongues, my heart overflowing with praise. The same doctor who had been so generous was right there, praying alongside me. It was a powerful moment, a reminder that even in the most challenging circumstances, God's presence was unmistakable and that He would strategically put his servants in place to support His children. The day after surgery, I felt like I had gone ten rounds with Mike Tyson, but he won! My body ached, and I could barely keep my eyes open. But as I cautiously opened my left eye, the world burst forth in brilliant colors—like a newborn baby seeing for the first time. It was an awe-inspiring moment, a flicker of hope that felt almost miraculous. However, that evening, the excitement turned to panic as I experienced a sudden onset of glaucoma. I was rushed back into surgery, my heart racing with fear. When I awoke again, the results were mixed. I could see, but not as clearly as the day before.

Faith While Waiting

Now, I was being prepared for surgery on my left eye, which was in worse condition than my right. The first eye doctor had referred me to a specialist who dealt with severe cases, and I braced myself for what was to come with this battle with blindness.

With each challenge, I reminded myself of the words I had clung to so tightly: *"Lord, I trust You, I trust You Lord!"* Even as I faced uncertainty, I felt God's guiding hand, reminding me that this journey was not just about my sight; it was about faith, resilience, and the unwavering belief that miracles still happen, even in the darkest moments, and I was in a dark moment.

Reflecting on the day that the "Lights Went Out", I know realize it was not just an ending but a transformative beginning. While I mourned the loss of my sight, I also discovered a newfound depth to my existence in the Kingdom of God. My blindness became a part of my testimony—a chapter filled with lessons of sacrifice, resilience, love, and faith.

In the stillness of my heart, I began to understand that even in darkness, there is light. I recalled 2 Corinthians 5:7: *"For we walk by faith, not by sight."* This verse became my mantra, a reminder that faith could illuminate even the darkest challenges that I might be faced with.

The day it went dark marked a profound turning point in my life. Though I may never regain my physical sight, I have learned to see the world in ways I never imagined. I choose to walk forward, guided by faith and the heartbeat of God, embracing the beauty that remains, even in shadows. In this new chapter of my life, I trust that my journey is far from over, and I look ahead with hope, and faith in the Father, knowing that even in darkness, I am never alone.

1. Lean on Faith and Find Strength in Spiritual Resources

When facing a moment of crisis, like sudden blindness or any unexpected challenge, grounding yourself in your faith or spiritual beliefs can provide comfort and direction. Turn to scriptures, prayers, or affirmations that have anchored you in the past. They can act as a source of strength and remind you that you are not alone, even in the darkest moments.

2. Build a Support Network

Don't be afraid to rely on your community, family, or spiritual leaders for support. Sharing your struggles with trusted individuals can not only lighten the burden but also open doors to unexpected help and resources. Whether it's emotional encouragement, financial aid, or logistical support, a strong network can be a lifeline during tough times.

3. Focus on What You Can Control and Adapt

In the face of drastic change, focusing on what you *can* control helps manage the sense of loss or uncertainty. Take small, practical steps to adapt to your new reality. For example, learn new ways to navigate your environment or find alternative methods to carry out your responsibilities. Embracing flexibility allows you to maintain a sense of purpose and regain independence, even if it looks different than before.

Jay T. Harrison, Sr.

Overseer Jay T. Harrison Sr. was born at Sacred Heart Hospital on May 25, 1968, and raised in Chester, Pennsylvania. He is the fourth of six children and the only son of the late Bishop James and Pastor Emeritus Lessie Harrison. Pastor Harrison, who was born into a ministry led family, was exposed early on with a rearing that stressed community service. Overseer Harrison is very close to his family and enjoys spending quality time with them.

Mr. Harrison has been married to his wonderful wife and the mother of his children Elder Crystal Harrison for twenty-six years. God has blessed them with eight children: Jay Timothy. Jr., Juanita, Jessika, Katyce Jones, Robert, Romesha, Micah, Mekhi and Seven grandchildren; Jeremiah, Jordan, Aden Isaiah, Jaziah, Dorae, and Joy.

Education is highly valued in the Harrison household, with both parents holding advanced degrees. Overseer Harrison attended private Christian schools throughout his academic career, graduating from St. James High School for Boys. Upon graduation, Overseer Harrison attended the Delaware County Institute of Training to become a Nurse's Assistant, where he graduated at the top of his class with honors. Upon relocating to Williamsburg, VA, he became employed by the Eastern State Hospital. After four years of service, a work-related injury caused him to retire. Upon retirement Overseer Harrison increased his involvement in the ministry while at New Life Family Church, serving as the Youth Pastor, a position which prepared him for God's next assignment.

Overseer Harrison was subsequently employed at the Richard Milburn School, which was an alternative educational facility for at-promise youth. The success of that position resulted in Pastor Harrison's promotion to the Williamsburg Department of Social Services working with "At Promise Youth." What began as a Prevention Coordinator ultimately advanced to the Community Services Director during His employment with the Williamsburg James City County Community Action Agency.

Overseer Harrison's passion for community activism extended beyond his employment. He became actively involved in the local NAACP and founded the Williamsburg Community Development Organization, which grew to more than twenty members. Overseer Harrison was also actively involved in the Youth Services Coalition where he served as Chairman of the Safe and Drug Free Schools Dropout Prevention Program, and co-founder of the Neighborhood Basketball League, which continues to serve students in the Williamsburg-James City County, York County, and surrounding localities.

In November of 1999, Rev. Jay T. Harrison Sr. was elected as the first African American Republican and only the second African American to serve on the Board of Supervisors of James City County VA. During his tenure in office Overseer Harrison served as President of the James City County Transit Company, Chairman and Vice-Chairman of the JCSA, Chairman and Vice-Chairman of the James City County Board of Supervisors and the Regional Issues Committee, and two terms as Chairmen of the Greater Hampton Roads Workforce Development Board.

Overseer Harrison's ministerial experience began via his active involvement with his parent's ministry while growing up. Pastor Harrison has served as a Youth Pastor at New Life Family Church located in Williamsburg, Virginia and was the founding Pastor of Living Word Mission. Also having served as the Youth Pastor at Green Springs Chapel he subsequently served as an Elder at Resurrection House International Ministries, and successively founded Keys for Change Family Life Ministries.

Upon his return to Chester, PA he served as Co-Pastor of the True Vine Missionary Full Gospel Baptist Church (MFGBC) under the leadership of his mother, the Rev. Lessie L. Harrison since 2004. He has also founded the Keys For Change Community Development Corporation, the purpose of which is to develop families into strong "Kingdom Citizens" by offering a Marriage Enrichment Ministry, Leadership Training, and the "5 Days of Grace" Healing and Deliverance Crusade.

Overseer Harrison is actively involved in the Full Gospel Baptist Church Fellowship where he currently serves as the State Director of Intercessory Prayer for the region. Overseer Harrison was elevated to the position of Eastern District Overseer for the State of Pennsylvania where he oversees several churches. Overseer Harrison is the founder of Churches United for Harvest. The Keys for Change Sons & Daughters Ministerial Alliance was recently established to provide covering, mentorship and accountability for the licensed and ordained clergy birthed into a ministry leadership role and for those that call him their spiritual father.

True Vine MFGB Church has re-established its weekly bible studies in Philadelphia PA, New Castle Delaware, Penns Grove New Jersey. In 2012 Overseer released the vision for "Clear Direction Ministries" located in Williamsburg, Virginia under the leadership of his spiritual son and daughter Elder Alexander and Elder Elizabeth Butler.

Contact Information:

Website: www.keys4changeministries.com
Facebook: Overseer Jay T. Harrison Sr.
Email: Keys4change7@gmail.com

"Rejoice in hope, be patient in tribulation, be constant in prayer."
– Romans 12:12

Chapter Ten
Tanisha Graves
The Advocate's Heart

Now faith is confidence in what we hope for and assurance about what we do not see.
(Hebrews 11:1)

It is in the unpredictable times that your faith is tested. I was under a great amount of stress, taken out of work for medical issues, didn't have enough monies to pay my bills, I felt that the Lord didn't care about my needs. I cried many days and nights pleading for God to deliver me out of my situation and felt like my prayers fell on unfertilized ground. I would look around in silence while the tears saturated my skin and was reminded to hold on to my faith. It is in this season that I realized that faith is the evidence of things hoped for, evidence of things not seen.

After the devastating loss of suddenly losing my oldest son, I was faced with the following questions: What was my purpose? How would I go forth in life? How could I be an effective advocate and fight for the lives of others after I had lost my fight for him? How would I hold it together and be strong during a time when I was vulnerable, in disbelief, despair, and at a loss in so many ways?

I felt betrayed by the Lord as I felt He had not heard or answered my countless prayers for healing my son. I was torn and left without a purpose to go on.

Faith While Waiting

While waiting for answers talk and open up your heart to God. God moves in His timing and not ours. I'm still waiting on my full and complete break through to come as I endure through grief. I'm going to stay in prayer, read my Word and keep my Faith. I will not rush God as He will mold me into Who He would have me to be. So, Faith While Waiting is a process that we all must go through but be assured God knows exactly what He is doing with each one of us.

Waiting on a cure for some conditions may never come, but as a mother you never give up hope. In my sons case, a cure for his seizures never came. After fighting for nearly three decades, Marquis lost his battle to Epilepsy.

People have tried to sabotage and block me, slammed doors in my face, and spoke ill will over my life. But my weapon of defense is found in Galatians 6:9, that "if we faint not." Don't get tired in doing good. God sent me to a Judge to deliver this message that someone will have a seizure while entering into his courtroom. there will be nothing that he could do as he will be presiding over the court.. Guess what? Within two weeks or less the Judge informed me that a lady entering his courtroom had a seizure, hitting her and almost losing her life. He then said I need to train my staff and peers. My son would be so proud, as were given the opportunity to train WJJC Courts on seizure safety.. While I couldn't save Marquis, I thank God for the opportunity to save others!

We hear this cliché, *prayer changes things more often than not,* but I am a living witness that this is truth because it has worked in my favor. I would advise everyone to spend an intimate time with the Lord. Find a quiet place where you can pour your heart out to him and wait for His answers. Surround yourself with positive people, "as iron sharpens iron" (Proverbs 27:17).

The Bible instructs us to "Wait on the Lord and be of good courage (Psalms 27:14). When your faith is tested "Lean not on your own understanding" trust God during the process. It may not seem like it but there's a purpose.. **While waiting** read your Word, apply it your life and ask God to lead you. Gods response to me was Jeremiah 29:11, "For I know the plans I have for you," declares the LORD, "plans to prosper you and not to harm you, plans to give you hope and a future.

The Bible explains that "Faith is the substance of things hoped for, the evidence of things not seen (Hebrews 11:1). I am expecting something good to happen as my effort, dedication, and determination while waiting in the maturation process. If you have faith as a grain of a mustard seed… then nothing is impossible for you (Matthew 17:20).

Faith moves and gives us the courage to venture into the unknown. It's a conviction that takes custody and assures us of God's promises. God provided a platform where we speak about grief and how to deal with it. Talking openly about your grief opens you up for healing. I encourage you to not "Let not your heart be troubled" for trouble won't last always. Do not focus on what is before you but the Words that God has given. Reminisce on the many blessings, count and store them up in your heart. 1 Peter 2:9-10 says,

> You are a chosen people, a royal
> priesthood, a holy nation, God's special
> possession, that you may declare the
> praises of him who called you out of
> darkness into his wonderful light. Once

> you were not a people, but now you are
> the people of God; once you had not
> received mercy, but now you have
> received mercy

In my waiting, I advocated for my son's medical treatment and later became a voice for other families that were standing in need of help. After losing my son, God showed me His plans to restore me. God opened doors that others felt I shouldn't be. I had no qualifications. In the beginning people shamed, mishandled, and misused me. They even talked ill about me. I had to draw closer to God so that my Faith would

    Story of King David his son by Uriah became sick. So David fasted and laid down on the ground at night. The servants were afraid to tell David that his son had died. David saw his servants whisper together and then understood that the child had died. David arose from the ground, washed up changed his and anointed himself. He went into the Lord house then to his house and ate. The servants asked what is this thing that you have done? David later said he is now dead, why should I fast? I shall go to him and he shall not return to me (2 Samuel 12:15-23)

    This scripture reminded me that Gods will for your life is His will and not mine. We all have an appointed time to return back to the Father.

    The Prophet Elisha wanted a double portion (2 Kings 2:9), that only God could give. In 2 Corinthians 4:16-18, the Apostle Paul encourages Christians to not lose heart, "For which cause we faint not..." The word "faint" refers to "a failing of the heart" or giving up. Paul said regardless of what comes his way, he won't give up.

We are challenged with problems of this world but should stay focused on Gods promises. In the coming world nothing compares to "the glory that shall be revealed in us..

The outer self is wasting away, and our inner self is renewed day by day. It is only a momentary affliction that is preparing us for eternal glory. Look not to things that are seen but to the things that are unseen. For the things seen are transient, but the things unseen are eternal.

The Holy Spirit guides our steps, provides peace and joy in every situation. Renewing our inward man means knowing that this world is not our home.

In the Book of Psalms 40:1-4, Moses explains

> 1 I waited patiently for the LORD;
>   he inclined to me and heard my cry.
> ² He drew me up from the pit of destruction,
>   out of the miry bog,
> and set my feet upon a rock,
>   making my steps secure.
> ³ He put a new song in my mouth,
>   a song of praise to our God.
> Many will see and fear,
>   and put their trust in the LORD.

> [4] Blessed is the man who makes
> the LORD his trust,
> who does not turn to the proud,
> to those who go astray after a lie!

Everyone knows the trials and tribulations as well as the victories and exhalations during Moses time. He had the privilege of appearing with Christ as He revealed His heavenly glory to select disciples while still on earth. I have been fortunate to be a recipient of His heavenly glory as well while here on earth and it inspires me to keep on pressing even with the mind, body, and sometimes spirit say no.

Eagle eye readiness:
1. Don't give up
2. Stay focused
3. The reward is greater than the risk

Equip yourself by:
1. Read your Bible
2. Praying without ceasing
3. Meditate (Chew) on the Word of God

Encourage Yourself:
1. Speak Positive things into existence
2. Align yourself with like-minded believers
3. Pray in and out of season

Minister Tanisha Tyler Graves

Tanisha Tyler Graves is a renowned Epilepsy and Seizure Awareness advocate, the author of "I Pulled the Sun out for You", and Co – Author of the Amazon Best Seller book– "Moments for Moms Vol II." She is a minister, wife, mother, and grandmother who has a great love for God, family, and the well-being of others. The love she shares for others was intensified after the loss of her first-born son who passed away suddenly on September 2, 2019. During bereavement, she contemplated giving up, but God had other plans, explaining, "I'm going to use you, my child, for My Glory." Minister Graves now spends her time pouring and encouraging others as an Evangelist giving testimonies about what the Lord has done for her and what He is capable of doing for them as well.

She faithfully serves her local communities and abroad, speaking on behalf of the voiceless, their families, and those impacted by health disparities. In addition, she assists the government with investigating and researching ways to improve the quality of life of those suffering from Seizure-related brain trauma. This fall, Minister Graves will be furthering her ministerial calling by enrolling in the Williamsburg Theological Seminary Doctorate program in Biblical Counseling and graduating in 2025.

Contact Information:

Website: TanishaTylerGraves.com
Wtts4epilepsy.org
Operationloveinc.org
Facebook: Tanisha Graves

"The Lord is good to those who wait for him, to the soul who seeks him."

– **Lamentations 3:25**

Chapter Eleven

Lisa Seymour

A Blessing In the Wait

But, on the contrary, as the Scripture says, What eye has not seen and ear has not heard and has not entered into the heart of man, [all that] God has prepared (made and keeps ready) for those who love Him [who hold Him in affectionate reverence, promptly obeying Him and gratefully recognizing the benefits He has bestowed]

. *1 Corinthians 2:9 (AMPC)*

Waiting is never easy, nor is it fun. Many emotions and thoughts race through your head as you sit in the waiting period while trying to hold on to your faith. Being a minister of the gospel or person of faith doesn't mean you are exempt from going through situations where you are going to have to lean on your faith during the waiting season, even when you can't see how that thing is going to work out. There has been many points in my life where I had to lean on my faith while waiting for God to do it again, but the one that stands out is waiting for the door to open for me to return to the not-for-profit field.

Thirteen years ago, I did something that should have caused me to lose everything, my family, my freedom, and my mind but I didn't. I did suffer a consequence and that was I was removed from my passion of serving those in need of support, encouragement, and empowerment during their tough times and it seemed like I would never have that opportunity again. This season had broken me mentally, emotionally, and even spiritually. There were moments that I even became angry with God. Yes, the good Reverend got mad at God. I began to ask God, "Why did He not let me get what I deserved if I was going to have to struggle finding a job I qualified for?" If I hadn't learned by now to "Have Faith in the Process", this season definitely taught me.

Over the next two years, I began to accept positions that I was overqualified for because of the guilt and shame I carried due to my actions. The positions allowed me to reach people, but I knew that was not what I was supposed to do I would often find myself crying and asking God, "why was He letting this go on so long if He had forgiven me?" The impact that this was having on my family made me feel like ending it all so that they could live better, but how many know that your circle matters. If it wasn't for my husband and my covenant sisters, I would have given up the fight. My covenant sisters are those women that God has blessed me to have on this journey called life. They pray with and for me. They listen and encourage me when I needed. They push me to be all that God has called me to be and they hold me up when I don't have the strength to do so myself. My husband constantly spoke life in me and prayed over me. He would remind me every day that he was here for the journey. Seeing their faith in my breakthrough allowed me to change my mindset and I had a come to Jesus moment with myself, and I began to remember what I heard and not what see. I began to stand on the promise of Isaiah 55:11 (NIV), "So is My Word that goes out from My mouth: It will not return to Me empty, but will accomplish what I desire and achieve the purpose for which I sent it." I got my fire back and I stopped applying and accepting positions that I know I was overqualified for, and stepped out on faith and applied for a position that I didn't have all of the qualifications for but it would put me in position to do what I love to do. You know that the position didn't come easy. I interviewed in October and was told that I would hear back in a week. A week turned into a month, but I kept hearing hold on. I am so glad I didn't throw in the towel because I got the job! If I would have given up, I would have missed out on all that God had waiting for me on the other side.

This was a pivotal moment in my faith journey because it taught me that the waiting room of life is sometimes necessary for where you are going and also sometimes we create our own waiting room due to our lack of faith. Well what do you mean Lady Lisa? Well I am glad you asked. Sometimes it is necessary for us to sit in the waiting room to ensure that what we are waiting on is ready for us and we are ready for it. If you find yourself in a waiting period let me encourage you to not give up in the wait. Instead of looking at how long it's taking, think "What God is about to do is going to blow my mind!" When we change our perspective on how we wait, the waiting becomes easy.

One of the most important ingredients to having faith and patience while you wait, is to often recall how God showed up before and when He did, it was right on time. Another key ingredient is spending time mediating on the Word that is full of testimonies of people just like you and me who experienced a waiting season and it worked for their good, and God's glory. Lastly, get you a community who can stand with you in faith. You were never meant to go through your challenge by yourself. Ask God to connect you with your community and watch Him send you the people you need.

I leave you with this promise from your Father: Matthew 9:29 (NLT) Then He touched their eyes and said, "Because of your faith, it will happen." I believe with you!

Practical Tips to Keep in the Waiting Room of Life:

Lean into God: The most common thing for us to do when it feels like the wait is to long is turn from God. Leaning into God through prayer and His Word will allow you to find strength and peace while you wait for Him to answer because He will.

Stay Connected: One of the biggest lessons I have learned during my waiting period is that community is important. Not just any community, but one that can pray for and with you, hold you accountable, and speak life.

Keep It Moving: One of the most misconceptions of faith is it is just something we have, but in fact it produces action. As you wait on God, keep moving forward on purpose and in purpose. This will help you see that even through the rough times, "I'm Still Chosen."

Lisa Seymour

Lady Lisa Seymour serves as an Associate Minister at Logan Street Baptist Church under the leadership of her husband, Dr. David J. Seymour. Lisa is the Founder of Broken 2 Be Blessed Ministries, LLC and released her first book, After The Fall, in December of 2022 and an updated version, After the Fall 2.0 in February of 2023 and will release her next book, a 21-day devotional, titled I Said What I Said Signed, God: Moving from Fear to Faith in 2024. Lisa co-authored a book last summer with four other women to share their stories of dealing with the loss of a child.

Lady Lisa is a Spiritual Midwife, Author, Speaker, and Teacher. She enjoys mentoring young women ages 18-35 as they find their identity and purpose in Christ. Lady Lisa facilitates a weekly virtual Bible Study that includes young women from Texas, Iowa, Florida, and Illinois. Lady Lisa is gearing up to host the first annual "Healing Her Within: Soul Care Edition conference August 17, 2025. This conference is one that will provide a courageous space for women to release the weight they have been carrying for far too long from undealt with traumas of their past or present so they will be healed and whole to enjoy life to the fullest.

Lady Lisa continues her passion to serve and spread the Gospel through her role as an Associate Executive Director of Program Support for a Private Child Welfare Service Agency in Illinois. Lady Lisa knows that she has been called to extend grace and mercy, and speak life to those whom the world has deemed as unfit to be used for great things in the kingdom.

Lady Lisa holds a Masters of Divinity with an emphasis in Pastoral Care from Northern Seminary. Lisa is currently completing her Mental Health and Life Coaching Certificates, and will begin her doctoral program in the fall of 2024 at McCormick Theological Seminary.

Lady Lisa is a proud member of Delta Sigma Theta Sorority, Inc. where she actively services her community by participating and donating to the Annual DeKalb Back to School Bash and providing resources to local middle schools to hand out to teenage girls in need. Lady Lisa has also served her community by responding to the ask for monetary or clothing donations to aid a family in need.

Lady Lisa lives in Dekalb, IL with her husband and their amazing son, David Christian.

Contact Information:

Email: lisa.seymour5@gmail.com
Website: www.broken2beblessedministries.com
Facebook: @Broken2BeBlessedMinistries

"Now faith is the substance of things hoped for, the evidence of things not seen."
-*Hebrews 11:1*

Chapter Twelve
Tonya B. Bailey

Tested Faith

"Trust God even when it seems dark, your faith will bring light to your darkness. Focus on God and do not give up."

The summer I turned eleven, everything in my world shifted. It was the year I learned what it truly meant to wait. Up until then, life had followed a predictable rhythm. I was raised in a small town by my grandmother Maggie Drummond after my mother Otelia Bagwell passed when I was only three years old. My grandmother always made sure I was well taken care of and had everything I needed and wanted. I was surrounded by a close-knit family; I have five sisters and two brothers.

My normal day growing up looked like- church, school, friends, family gatherings. After I turned eleven, I became ill, and doctor's visits became a part of that rhythm. The illness I developed caused my kidneys function to decline. This resulted in more frequent doctor's visits. At that age, I did not understand what was happening in my life, but I soon realized that I would have to make decisions on how I was going to make it.

I was growing up and trying to do teenage things, but my health would not allow me to. At fourteen years old, I ended up on dialysis for about 5 years, until I received my transplant. I went on to attend college in Virginia Beach. My grandmother died while I was in college; that broke me down because she was my heart and soul. I still managed to graduate with my associate's degree, even while dealing with grief of losing my grandmother and facing my own health issues. After I completed school, I moved back to my hometown and began working as a Nursing Assistant. I felt like I was alone because the one person that I really loved had died. I had other family, but there is no one like your mom or grandmother who will do anything for you. I was dating but our lives were not right, and I knew that God was not going to bless us. Yes, I had been going to church all my life, but I still did not understand what God was doing in my life.

My grandmother raised me to be independent, so I knew what I needed to survive. I started working at the local hospital as a phlebotomist and continued to advance in my education. After dating for a while, I got married and I continued to work and was presented with the opportunity to become a Support Service Supervisor. Now, that was something big for me, because I always wanted to be a leader. This gave me a chance to learn new things. As I continued to work, going to church regularly to worship God, I began to see the blessings that God had bestowed upon me. Just when you think your life is going well, something happens. My faith became tested again when I was told that I needed another transplant, and I was not too happy about that. I became upset and stressed because I was not sure what had happened. I always knew in my heart that my transplant would one day stop working because it did not belong to me, but I never really thought it would be now. So, my world was about to come crumbling down. I had so many questions but not getting the answers I wanted to hear. Yes, I can say that I have kept this transplant for 30 years which is a long time for some. I do not want to say I went into a depression state. I just found myself in a place of darkness. I had to figure out ways of changing my eating habits, resting more, and giving up some things. My transplant is still working but it is declining. Yes, I would sit in church just going through the motions, by my mind was not there. I would cry out, attitude would be overwhelming, mind all over the place, trying to figure things out myself. I began to pray and read but that was not helping me, at least that what I thought. As the years passed, I was put on the list for another transplant, which is good. So, I began feeling better about the situation, changed my attitude, and began

Faith While Waiting

thanking God for what was about to go about your business. Humm, I just knew that my new transplant was on the way, BUT GOD had another plan. God will give you a test to see how well you can manage it. I was the top of the list for a transplant, but then I ended up with Stage Breast Cancer and now I must wait five years. My faith was tested once again, and my focus was on what I was going through and not God. I questioned God, cried out, told my family, but a few days past, I begin to think about what God had done for me thus far. The song by Yolanda Adams, *The Battle is Nor Yours it is The Lord* is one of favorite songs it came to mind, it really speaks to me about allowing God to be God and let Him do what He said He would do. Sometimes you forget who God is when you are going through something, and you do not realize he is the one you need. I was not going to let this test break me. I had to find a way to get back to God, so I started writing a prayer journal, *Pray Without Ceasing.* One of my prayers that comes to mind is, Pray for Breakthrough, "God, I thank you for giving me this test. God allow me to come out of this on top. God, I pray that you will take all my flaws with no judgement." (Bailey, 8). In writing this journal, it has really helped me get back to knowing God and who He is, and I am learning to have patience and faith while waiting for my blessing to come. I know God is keeping me through all of this and will not leave me or forsake me. I am here for a reason and a purpose, and I want nothing more than to fulfill the purpose God has for me because at the end God gets the glory.

In waiting for God to bless you, pray, read, worship Him even when things do not look like they are working, and keep the faith. Your praise will not go unnoticed, God sees all and knows your heart.

Faith While Waiting

Tonya Bailey

Tonya Bailey, a resident of Virginia's Eastern Shore, has been happily married to her husband Craig for eight years. Though she does not have children of her own, she is a proud stepmother to three stepchildren and a loving grandmother to nine step-grandchildren. Tonya was raised in Boston, Virginia, by her grandmother, following the passing of her mother when she was just two years old—a loss that has been softened by frequent reminders of how much she resembles and reflects her mother.

Her childhood was largely positive, despite some health challenges. Today, she is a 30-year transplant recipient and a breast cancer survivor, demonstrating her resilience and faith. Tonya works at the local hospital as a Support Services Supervisor and Phlebotomist. Her faith journey has always been a cornerstone of her life; she grew up attending church every Sunday and remains an active member of Shiloh Baptist Church. There, she serves as a Deaconess, sings in the choir, and is involved in both the decoration and outreach ministries. Tonya holds a bachelor's degree in Health Management/Administration and an MBA. She is also a passionate podcaster, hosting two shows: *Journey of a Kidney Survivor* and *Pushing to Your Purpose*. In addition to her podcasts, she is the author of *Pray Without Ceasing*, a 31-day prayer journal filled with her personal prayers and scriptures. This journal was born out of a period of health struggles when her faith was put to the test, leading her back to God through writing and prayer. One of her favorite scriptures is Isaiah 54:17: "No weapon formed against thee shall prosper; and every tongue that shall rise against thee in judgment thou shalt condemn."

Tonya enjoys dancing, reading, writing, and spending quality time with her family. Although public speaking has never come naturally to her, she is stepping out of her comfort zone with her current projects and is eager for new, exciting experiences. She finds peace in the assurance that God remains faithful and will fulfill His promises.

Contact Information:

Website: Tonya.bailey89@yahoo.com
Facebook: tonya b bailey
Instagram: tonya_b_bailey

***"Waiting time is not wasted time when it's in God's hands." –
Anonymous***

Chapter Thirteen
Juanita N. Woodson
Finding Purpose in the Wait

"Consider it pure joy, my brothers and sisters, whenever you face trials of many kinds, because you know that the testing of your faith produces perseverance. Let perseverance finish its work so that you may be mature and complete, not lacking anything."

James 1:2-4 (NIV)

Waiting is never easy, but it does build endurance when you have trust and faith in God. When you hear the words that it will be difficult to birth another child that is one of the most gut-wrenching feelings, especially when you have finally done things the right way. April10th, 2022, I was so happy when the pregnancy test came back as positive. I was even happier to share the results with my husband. I will never forget the pure bliss that we experienced after finding out that we were bringing a child into this world, together. Our blended family would really be blended now.

All of that changed on April 19th. I began experiencing the worst pain ever. I was literally on the floor in pain. My husband rushed home from work and we went to the emergency room. We waited for what seemed like an eternity. While waiting, I was praying. Lord, please don't let there be anything wrong with my baby. After hours of waiting, I was finally taken back for tests, an ultrasound and then sent home to see how I feel the next day. I will save the way I was treated in the hospital for another book. The next day, I found myself literally having to crawl from the kitchen back to our bedroom in the worst pain ever, I knew this was not okay. In that moment, I did not want my son to come out

Faith While Waiting

of his room and see me lying on the floor in pain, so I had to make my way back there.

The amount of pain that I faced and not being able to move resulted in the ambulance coming and ultimately being transported. I was back at the same hospital, waiting. They finally told us that we were losing the baby and I needed to have immediate surgery. I was facing internal bleeding. I was transported to another hospital that was better equipped to help me. Not only was I in the worst pain ever, my heart was broken. April 20th, 2022, changed my life forever. But I decided that I would still trust that God would give us His promises.

I am still in the waiting period. Going through that experience tested my faith on different levels. To finally have an answered prayer and then it gets snatched away from you can make you want to shut down. If it was not for my foundation in God and the constant reminders He has sent me that He has plans to prosper and not harm me, I don't know where I would be. Fast forward, I have experienced two back-to-back surgeries, blood transfusions and months of pain. All of these things could have broken me and just caused me to doubt that God was going to do anything, let alone allow me to bring another child into this world with my husband.

When your mind is fixated on one thing, it can make it hard to move forward and walk in your purpose. While I have not given up hope of having another child, my mind is stayed on the call God has on my life. Writing has been a major coping mechanism for me and also building a community to pour into others.

The waiting season tested my faith in ways I hadn't anticipated. After the miscarriage and surgeries, it would have been easy to fall into despair. I often found myself asking, Why, God? Why after praying and waiting for so long? Why after doing things the "right" way? But in those moments of questioning, I realized my faith had to grow deeper, not just as a belief in what I wanted but as trust in God's bigger plan. I learned that faith isn't just about receiving blessings but learning to trust God in the midst of heartache and uncertainty.

During this time, my strength came from God's Word. One scripture that became an anchor for me was Jeremiah 29:11: "For I know the plans I have for you," declares the Lord, "plans to prosper you and not to harm you, plans to give you hope and a future." It reminded me that even though I couldn't see it, God had a future for me, one filled with hope.

Books like 'Do It Anyway' by Tasha Cobbs-Leonard also helped me find comfort. She shared how even in the midst of struggle, God's purpose for us remains. Her words helped me find strength in my waiting.

There was one moment in particular that became a turning point for me. After months of pain and waiting, I felt God whisper to my heart: I'm doing something new in you. It wasn't about the baby I had lost, though the grief remained, but about a deeper work God was doing in me. He was transforming my heart and teaching me endurance. This was not about losing faith; it was about building it. Every tear, every prayer, was shaping my trust in Him. I realized I had been holding onto my plan so tightly, but God was asking me to surrender, to trust Him with the outcome.

The situation didn't resolve the way I had originally hoped, at least not yet. The dream of another child is still in my heart, but I've learned that God's timing and purposes often look different than our own. While I am still in the waiting period, this experience shifted my focus from solely waiting for another child to living out my calling now. Writing, encouraging others, and embracing my purpose have become part of the healing journey.

The journey has changed me in profound ways. I've learned to lean into God, even when the answers aren't clear. I've learned patience and endurance—two things I thought I had mastered but discovered there were deeper levels to both. Through the surgeries, pain, and waiting, God taught me to find joy in the present and trust Him for the future. This experience has deepened my faith, allowing me to see God not just as a provider of the things I want but as the sustainer of my soul. I now understand that waiting is part of God's process for refining us. It's uncomfortable and at times painful, but it strengthens the roots of our faith. I now see waiting as an active process, where God is working even when we can't see it.

To anyone in a season of waiting, I want you to know this: God is faithful, even when we don't understand His timing. It's okay to feel frustrated or disappointed, but don't let go of your hope. God hasn't forgotten you, and He never wastes a season…even a season of waiting. He is preparing something far greater than you can imagine.

1. Stay connected to God's Word: Find scriptures that speak to your situation and meditate on them daily. They will give you strength when you feel weak.

2. Surround yourself with support: Don't isolate yourself in the waiting. Find a community of believers who can pray with you and remind you of God's promises.

3. Keep moving forward in your purpose: Even while you wait, God has work for you to do. Focus on the calling He has given you today, and trust that He is taking care of tomorrow.

4. Journal your journey: Writing has been a huge part of my healing. It's a way to process the pain and also to look back and see how far God has brought you.

Juanita N. Woodson

Juanita N. Woodson, a devoted wife and nurturing mother, stands as a beacon of inspiration in both her personal and professional life. As a best-selling author, skillfully woven her testimony into books that captivate the hearts and minds of readers around the world.
In addition to her literary accomplishments, Juanita is the visionary owner of Grace 4 Purpose Publishing Co. LLC. With a passion for empowering others, she dedicates her time to coaching aspiring authors, guiding them on their journey to not only write but also successfully publish their own stories. Her commitment to nurturing the creative spirit within each individual is reflected in the diverse and impactful works that emerge under her guidance.

Faith While Waiting

Beyond the realm of publishing, Juanita is a multifaceted entrepreneur who seamlessly balances the roles of mentor, leader, and advocate. Her dedication to the written word is matched only by her commitment to fostering a community where aspiring writers can flourish and find their voices.

In her journey to leave an indelible mark on the literary landscape, Juanita N. Woodson continues to inspire, uplift, and empower those around her, leaving an enduring legacy of creativity, resilience, and purpose.

Contact Information:

Email: contact@grace4purposeco.com

Instagram: @_juanitanicole_

Facebook: Juanita Nicole Woodson

Website: www.grace4purposeco.com

Faith While Waiting

www.grace4purposeco.com

Faith While Waiting

www.ingramcontent.com/pod-product-compliance
Lightning Source LLC
Chambersburg PA
CBHW072155160426
43197CB00012B/2396